T0209348

Silent Tears
A Journey of Faith

Nancy Umberger

WestBow Press books may be ordered through booksellers or by contacting:

WestBow Press
A Division of Thomas Nelson & Zondervan
1663 Liberty Drive
Bloomington, IN 47403
www.westbowpress.com
1 (866) 928-1240

ISBN: 978-1-9736-4229-9 (sc)
ISBN: 978-1-9736-4230-5 (hc)
ISBN: 978-1-9736-4228-2 (e)

Library of Congress Control Number: 2018912084

Print information available on the last page.

WestBow Press rev. date: 10/9/2018

Introduction

I guess there's something to be said for the power of words. According to Proverbs 18:21 (ESV), "Death and life are in the power of the tongue." This is a statement we should heed. Knowing when to speak is a challenge for me as I think it is for most people. I never thought my words carried the power of death. I wondering whom I have murdered with my words or brought to the brink of death. Whom have I pushed over the edge or caused to stumble because of my inability to choose my words wisely or my lack of control over my tongue?

I know we can all relate to what I have just said, and we can think of a few people in our own homes we have injured—maybe not put to death. If I stop here, I feel defeated since I know I have injured a lot of people in my life. We know 1 John 1:9 can help us with the defeat we feel since God is always willing to forgive; therefore, God allows us to make amends with those we have wounded. One thing we need to remember is that wounds often carry scars, so it may take work on our part to prove ourselves.

As the story goes—and I have no idea where this originated—a young boy had trouble controlling his words not only with siblings but also with friends. His parents watched this happen repeatedly but couldn't get him to stop being cruel with his words. His name-calling finally reached a point that his siblings and friends were hurt beyond repair.

His dad decided to take action. He told the boy each time he called someone a name or said anything hurtful, he was to go outside and place a nail in the fence post. The nails accumulated each day. Finally, the dad told the boy that there was a way he could remove them—the boy had to apologize each time he hurt someone with his words. Then and only then could he go out and remove one nail. Over time, the young boy pulled out all the nails, but to his surprise, the fence post looked hideous with all those nail holes. His dad explained that spoken words were like the sharp point of a nail driven deep in others' hearts. Though the apology is given and the nail is removed, the damage has been done.

Life lesson learned? You bet. Words are powerful.

Teaching our children this important concept is a challenge especially if we struggle with that problem ourselves. We all like to say we have issues, but why don't we call them what they are? Sin. Anger is not an issue; it is a sin problem. Hurting others with our words is not an issue or something we cannot help. It is sin. We all need a reminder every now and again that we use the world's lingo—"I have an issue" or "I can't help the way I react. I have a bad temper." But in reality, we need to say, "I have sin in my life, and only God can help me through it." Harsh words I know. Believe me; the power of my own words is convicting.

You may think I am obsessed with words, but I am on a new adventure in my life, and words have been the focal point. Words are a very important part of our lives. On the average, from what I could find, we use between 12,000 and 18,000 words each day. Some of us use more and others less, but it's interesting to see numbers. I know I talk a lot—probably a lot more than the numbers I have shown. This has made me wonder how many of my words are deadly poison and how many are sweet honey?

My life seems to take many twists and turns. I always say, "There's never a dull minute at my house." I prefer to think of these twists and turns as adventures rather than annoyances because life's annoyances don't have the same effect as adventures do. Adventures carry life lessons; annoyances make us impatient or angry. I invite you to join me on my adventure of words to see their power including how you and I can change not only our lives but also the lives of others by our words.

I love to hike. I enjoy looking at a trail map and finding which trail is fitting for the day and the time I have. If you have ever gotten one of these maps, you will find trails are marked by three words: *easy, moderate,* or *strenuous.* Easy trails are no challenge but are a fun romp in the woods. Moderate trails present a bit of a challenge; they give novice hikers a sense of accomplishment and seasoned hikers a time to reflect on the beauty around them. Strenuous trails are a challenge. You must pay more attention and create ways to often get from point A to point B. Obviously, you wouldn't start a novice hiker on a trail marked strenuous.

We all start at different places in our lives. Trials are a lot like trail maps; many trails are marked easy, others moderate, and a few strenuous. The trail I have before me is marked strenuous. You must be wondering how words fit into this. Well, Proverbs 25:11 (NASB) answers this question: "Like apples of gold in settings of silver is a word spoken in right circumstances." According to this verse, we are given the challenge to choose our words either for death or life.

My backpack has all I need for a hike up Monument Mountain. That's a great name for a strenuous trail, don't you think? Even the name *Monument Mountain* gives the idea of something huge, gigantic. I have my map in my hand, and the strenuous trail has been highlighted for me. I will be following the red squares throughout my hike. The colored squares keep me focused and on the right trail. Different colors and shapes mark the other trails.

So dear friend, let's get started.

Trail Marker 1
October 29, 2011

Mammogram. That part of the trail was pretty easy. Just a yearly thing. I needed to go and have it done, and then the rest of the day belonged to my friend Rosa. That day was one of the best days of my life. I had my first pedicure, a fine lunch, and a friend day beyond belief. What a wonderful experience for my birthday. I felt like royalty. Not knowing what was ahead, God allowed Rosa to use her gift of words to build me up that day. It was the best day ever!

Trail Marker 2
November 1, 2011

I received a phone call that I had to get another mammogram. Okay. I'd had that happen before, so I made an appointment for the next day.

Trail Marker 3
November 2, 2011

A mammogram was done again. As I sat in the waiting room trying to be patient while the doctor read the X-ray, I knew in my heart that something wasn't right. That feeling was confirmed when Dr. Greene informed me that he had spotted something, maybe calcification. Because the calcification was in a line, it was a cause for concern. I needed to see a surgeon.

I left the office in shock. How could I have just had such a good time on Friday and then be faced with having to see a surgeon? I had to tell this news to the people I loved. They were words that needed to be spoken, but I could hardly speak. I called my husband. What could he say except "I'm sorry"?

I sent a text to my dear friend. I could not even speak. I saved the text she sent at 8:30 a.m.: "I'm so sorry." Words that showed compassion, not anger. Another text, at 8:44 a.m., read, "Let's keep sharpening each other." Those were words of courage spoken at a time when I was afraid and possibly she was too. Proverbs 27:17 (NASB) reads, "Iron sharpens iron, so one man sharpens another." That had been our friendship verse since the summer.

Another friend had to be told—my closest and dearest friend, Christy. Instantaneously, verses titled "Peace" came to me via email. Many verses echoed the peace God could give during storms in our lives. I had to tell family, which was the hardest. The unknown was so hard to explain. I cried. Silent tears drenched my face, but they were masterfully collected by a God who saw them and heard them.

I had to tell my son. How would I tell the child I had prayed for six years to have? I picked him up from school and told him the news. With those loving blue eyes, he said, "It'll be okay. If you die, I'll see you again." There wasn't any more discussion on the matter. He felt a peace and obviously had hope.

The last people I called were my parents—special people. They believed in the power of prayer. We prayed over the phone asking God to heal me but ultimately to have His will in my life—whatever that might be.

Trail Marker 4
November 3, 2011

I had an appointment with the surgeon at 11:00 a.m. Dr. Dasher was so kind to me. He explained to me that anytime calcification ran in a line, it ran the risk of being cancer, so a biopsy would be necessary. Surgery was scheduled for November 8. His partner, Dr. Nick Teppara, would do the surgery. I met him that morning.

I was not sure how I felt at that moment because I was numb. *Biopsy, linear line, cancer*—all these words were running rampant in my mind, but I couldn't make sense of what was happening because it was happening so fast. Every day, I searched scriptures for help, found comfort from friends, and prayed for my life.

Trail Marker 5
November 8, 2011

The day for my surgery. The first procedure was done at 7:45 a.m. That involved putting wire markers in my left breast to give accurate direction to the surgeon when he would remove the calcification.

The day was long, but my family and friends were there to give moral support. Leaving them was hard when I was wheeled into surgery. Again the unknown. I cried silent tears as my friend and family walked away.

I am exhausted. I've only started this hike, and yet my feet feel heavy as does my heart. I will rest here and continue to search for answers.

Trail Marker 6
November 16, 2011

I was to find out what the biopsy revealed that day. The door opened, and in walked Dr. Dasher and Dr. Teppara. My heart sank as Dr. Dasher sat beside me and said, "I have some good news and some bad. The good news is you have pre-cancer. The bad news is your left breast will have to be removed."

I couldn't believe what I was hearing—powerful words cutting through my heart.

He continued. "We believe the best course of action would be to remove both breasts. If we remove only one, you'd run the risk of cancer in the other and you'd have to be on medication for five years. We can do the double mastectomy and reconstructive all at one time. Do you have any questions?"

Questions? What could I say or ask at that moment? It happened before I could stop it—one tear fell to my cheek, and then another. Debra, the nurse, came in with a box of Kleenex. There sat the four of us while my tears fell. Appointments were made with the plastic surgeon and Dr. Teppara for the following week.

How would I tell anyone the words that had just been delivered to me? I sat in the parking lot and called my mother. She was such a prayer warrior for those who were hurting. I knew her prayers for me would storm the gates of heaven. I sent a text to Rosa but couldn't tell her; I just said it wasn't good news. I called Brian, my parents, and Christy. It wasn't long before a text came back—"You want to meet?" Yeah, I had to tell Rosa in person.

We met at Panera's at 11:00 a.m. We sat, and I told her the words I had heard earlier that day. We cried. She may never know the power of the words she chose that day when she said calmly, "Just get this done so we can do the things we want to do together, like fly." That statement may mean nothing to anyone, but to me, it meant everything. It was a statement of faith and friendship. We shed a few more tears together. Silent tears need no words. They are a universal language understood by friends.

My dearest friend, Christy, reiterated on the phone God's peace and power. She shared words of comfort with a sorrowful soul. Christy and I had been friends for more than twenty years. We've prayed each other through some tough things, so I knew she would pray.

Whew. The trail on Monument Mountain has been rough. The trail has had some steep inclines, but I have made it this far. In many ways, this has been the hardest trail I have ever been asked to climb. Along the trail, I have found ropes of friendship pulling me up when I was slipping, words of comfort that softened painful words received, and prayers offered when no words could be uttered.

I am resting here for a moment drinking in the beautiful scenery and reflecting on what God is trying to teach me on this adventure. I am resting in the words of my Savior and in the words others gave me along the way.

Though I've been on the trail for only a few weeks, at times, I've wondered if I could continue it. I feel numb. My mind can hardly conceive what is happening in my life. The tears keep coming day and night. Silent tears dripping, unheard to the human ear yet heard and collected by the Master. I ask the questions we all do—Why? Why now? Why me? I remind God of how hard this is for me. I don't think I can do this. I just want to be Jonathan's mom and Brian's wife. I want to be able to have coffee for a long time at Krankies, a favorite coffee shop, with my friend. The list of all the things I desire to do and the people I wanted to spend time with—more time with—grows.

Then I hear a voice, not a condescending or audible voice but a gentle and kind voice: "My grace is sufficient for you in times like these. I will walk with you each step of the way. My promises are true. I know the desires of your heart." Those words of comfort gave me a renewed strength to pick up my bag and keep climbing.

God, I know You love me, but there so many things I don't understand. Keep me near You on this trail. Make Yourself known to me daily. Help my friends who might be struggling with all this too. I love them so much, and they need You too. And God, please help my Jonathan have peace and learn to love You more through the storm we're facing. Please God.

Trail Marker 7
November 23, 2011

My name was finally called, and I went back. I was to meet the plastic surgeon that day. I'd been told he was one of the best. After meeting and chatting briefly, he told me what his part of the surgery would entail. He quizzed me on how I discovered my problem. I told him through a mammogram. I really hadn't discovered anything on my own. I told him that this was a shock. He asked, "How's your husband and son handling all this?"

My answer stunned him. "I don't know," I said. "I really don't know how either is doing. No one really wants to talk about it. This is a very sensitive matter. It happened so fast. I believe we're still processing the information. So really, everyone's at a different place in dealing with this news." Tears streamed down my face.

He was taken aback but not surprised. He could not believe my family was avoiding such an important issue, but he understood it. Everyone processes information like this in a different way. I assured him that was okay and that I'd figure things out.

He explained how his part in the surgery would inflict the most pain; he said I would require help after I got home. I must have looked like a deer in headlights when he said, "You'll have to ask for help the first week."

My mind went into overdrive. "Help? What kind of help?"

He explained that I'd have limitations when I got home. Tears again streamed down my face.

Judy, the patient coordinator, chimed in sweetly. "You don't ask for help, do you?" I couldn't answer. My life revolved around others, and I was the one who needed help. "What are you really worried about?" Judy asked. I began to explain what I felt, what I hadn't verbalized to too many yet felt obligated to do so then. "I don't think I can live without doing for others. What I mean is, I have children, not my own, who are in my home once or twice a week. They come to play with my son, and I'm there to serve them. We eat together, play together, and share problems and concerns. I don't want you to take that from me for a long time."

Telling a complete stranger about my fears was unnerving to say the least. I continued to ramble, and they listened. "You see, these children and their parents have become part of my life, like my own family. I just … I just want to be here for them for a long time."

There it was—laid bare, open for all to see.

"I just want to be here for a long time." Words ripped their way out of my heart and were exposed. "I just want to live to be with the ones who mean the most to me. I don't want to die."

All was quiet in the office except for my sniffling and tears. Dr. Willard was gentle as he said, "You'll be around for them for a long time. Let them help you so in time you can continue to do what you love." He told me how emotionally difficult this would be to go through. I was thankful for his honesty. It had already been an emotional ride for me. It had been challenging to cope with the tears, anger, hurt, and shock of the whole ordeal.

Strenuous trails are cumbersome. I found Trail Marker 7 to be extremely hard. I realize with each step taken, that my life on December 7 would change the dynamics of so many things. I'll have limitations for a couple of weeks, pain, new fears while waiting for more pathology reports, and relationships that would be affected forever—for the better or possibly for the worse. Emotionally, I have to prepare myself each day for these things. I believe God has given me doctors with the ability to be honest. Of course, I told them up-front to tell me the whole scenario. With such honesty comes my responsibility to prepare mentally for December 7.

I must stop at this point on the trail. Darkness falls. I find myself at a new stage in life. I have spoken words of truth to strangers and expressed what meant the most to me in life. I am so captivated by the love God so graciously gives me each day. I really don't deserve it. I find myself drawn to the book of Job. Job was a righteous man, yet God allowed Satan to sift him. Job 1:8 (ESV) reads, "And the Lord said to Satan, 'Have you considered my servant Job, that there is none like him on the earth, a blameless and upright man, who fears God and turns away from evil?'" Job was an outstanding man whose relationship with God was first and foremost. Can that be said of me? That my relationship with God is the most important thing in my life? I want it to be so, yet I know I fail Him often but He always draws me back to Him.

Job lost all he had including his health. Job had to wonder what God was doing in his life. He endured the strenuous trial God allowed in his life and came out a better person. Job 2:10 (NIV) reads, "Shall we accept good from God, and not trouble?" Now that's something to think on, isn't it? We all like it when good things happen, but what about troubles? Strenuous trails to climb? God is in control of the good and the bad. It is how I accept it that allows me to grow or be stunted in my spiritual growth. Emotionally, I am drained. I have cried until I am exhausted. Fatigue is creeping up on me, and I begin to feel sorry for myself.

Why now, God? Life seems to be on the upswing. I don't want to face any more doctors or decisions. I don't want this to happen. I want it to disappear. It's like a bad dream. O God, I need You to shed Your light in the darkness of my life. Help me please, God. Help all the pathology reports to be good. I am so incredibly afraid.

As I alluded to earlier, I had laid bare my words before strangers. What I said is now laid bare to all who read this. Words are so important. They express who we are, what we think, and how we cope with situations. I am thankful for the words in the Bible. They have been a source of comfort and companionship along the trail here on Monument Mountain. I want to say with Job, "I have treasured the words of his mouth more than my daily bread" (Job 23:12b NIV). I am thankful for the words of friends that have brought strength and stamina to me while each one of my steps has gotten harder and harder.

Trail Marker 8
November 28, 2011

I was riding with Rosa to take her parents to the airport. She and I planned to shop after that. I was thankful for that part of the trail. It was a wonderful day for me. We enjoyed each other's company. Words were exchanged. There were words, lots of them, explaining all the things I had heard in days past and words expressing my deepest fears—words. Then I heard her words, words of understanding, patience, and hope … soft words is a good description of them.

When the day was over and I found myself typing again, my heart filled with gratefulness for having such a friend in my life. I found a verse describing what my friend had done for me in the hours we had shared—Proverbs 15:4a (Voice): "A word of encouragement heals the one who receives it." Her words brought healing to where I hurt the most—my heart. We shopped and enjoyed the day to the fullest.

I wonder if we really know what a difference we can make in others' lives just by being available. If we could just for a few minutes choose to be unselfish and serve other people, would that make a real difference? I believe the answer is a resounding yes. Availability is so hard for each of us. Our schedules are inundated with appointments and events, but do we schedule time for availability? We never know when our schedules will call for us to be available for someone in need.

God, I thank You for my friends Rosa, Christy, Phyllis Brian, and my parents. Thank You for their availability and kind words, especially their words of hope. They may never know this side of eternity how their words have reached into the recesses of my heart and brought forth hope from a heart that lately has felt moments of despair. You have brought these people into my life for a reason. I love them all very much.

I ask in the stillness of the night that You bless them in a special way. I really don't have anything to offer them but my friendship and love. They are all so good to me. I never want to take their friendship for granted. Iron sharpens iron. Let us continue to sharpen each other in the days ahead. Lord, You know I need rest. Please provide that tonight. Let my mind be fixed on You. And God, thank You again for making today so special.

A new day and a restful night. I have been thinking about all the things God is teaching me throughout this adventure. One thing I have found is that God teaches me who He is in the midst of my trials. I heard a song before starting my adventure, and the words spoke directly to what I believe God was teaching me. It may be what He wants others to learn during this time as well. I want to move closer to God, not further away. It would have been easy to move away from God when He asked me to go on this strenuous trail, but my desire has been to rediscover Him in my life, to take my walk with Him to a different level.

I consider one song my theme song for how I want to live my life while I am on this adventure and when I come to the end of the trail/trial set before me.

"Let Me Rediscover You"
(Downhere)
How can I say I know you
When what I know is still so small?
Let me rediscover you and breathe in me your life anew
Tell me of the God I never knew
Oh, let me rediscover you.

What I put in bold print is my personal prayer each day that I will rediscover God in a fresh way and that He will breathe in me His life anew. Words whether sung or spoken have been my comfort.

As my surgery day approaches, I find myself listening carefully to words spoken, sung, and written. I am allowing my silent tears to fall freely knowing God has a plan for each tear.

Trail Marker 9
November 30, 2011

Another trip to the doctor's office. I was there for two hours, but it felt like eternity. I had so many questions. Dr. Teppara drew a picture for me of how he would do the mastectomy. Dr. Teppara told me the biopsy from the lymph node would be tested immediately and we would know right then if cancer was there or not. I was glad I wouldn't have to wait for days to hear something. He explained that pre-cancer was like having a baby cancer; it hadn't left the duct to become a devastating cancer. I hate that word—*cancer*—a destructive word that causes fear and pain.

He talked to me about my hospital stay, the concern of not being able to find a pain medication, what I would need when I came home, and what my limitations would be for a few weeks. He assured me he would take care of me every step of the way. The nurses all hugged me and told me how much they loved me and how my life had touched theirs.

I was moved to the next station, the surgery scheduler. I signed a bunch of papers and was given some papers to take home and read. I would wait for the hospital to call and tell me the time I needed to be there on December 7.

I left. I got in my car and just sat there for a minute trying to process all the information. Words had been spoken—a lot of them. That was the first time I hadn't cried. It was not because I was stronger or had come to accept the news and the surgery. I was numb. Hurt. Scared senseless. Overwhelmed. Not strong at all. I was sick of words that brought pain. I was sick of all of it! In seven days, my life would change forever. Not for a week or two but forever.

I was sure tears would come. Late at night when all was still, silent tears would pour like a dam unleashed. My pain centered on my family. I felt I was a burden to them. I understood we all grieved differently. Sometimes, there are no words to reveal the pain in our hearts. No one wants to discuss anything.

With just seven days left, I needed a listening ear. I prayed to have someone near me. It was so important to me then. I guess I was whining, not shining forth the love of Jesus, but I was hurting.

I get an email from Rosa. Funny, I read it around 10:00 p.m. after writing the above paragraph. The title of the devotional was "Put Your Heart into It," a devotional from 1 Thessalonians 5:17 (ESV) "Pray without ceasing." Words are powerful whether spoken or read. God used Rosa to send unspoken words to me at a time when no one but God knew where I was on my strenuous trail. A quote from this devotional really spoke to me: "The prayer that prevails is the prayer that is prayed with intensity—the prayer that is offered continually and passionately."

The trail is daunting. Moving yet not always knowing when to expect to see the next trail marker. I will wait here in the shadows and pray.

God, I feel fear rising up in me. The countdown is on. Just seven days. So many doctors to talk to, decisions I'm making alone. My family has emotionally checked out. God, please help me. Give me some kind of understanding in the midst of all this. I thank You for using Rosa in such a mighty way. Thank You for her obedience to send the email; she didn't have to. Help me pray for others with intensity. And passion. And compassion. Give me strength to continue to press on. Grant me rest. I'm mentally exhausted. Wrap Your blanket of peace around me tonight. Let me feel Your presence. I need You tonight.

Trail Marker 10
December 1, 2011

I had another doctor's appointment with Dr. Willard. I could not begin to pen how I felt. I was not ready to face surgery on December 7. Many words were spoken by the doctor and the nurses—words of concern because of all my medication allergies, words of compassion, and words of caution alluding to infection or overdoing things. Words bounced off the walls from every angle. I was informed of every cut, stitch, tube, and medication and how much help I would need. No stone left unturned. The words that hurt the most were, "You won't look normal when you look at yourself in a mirror."

The trail got steeper. I stared blankly into the full-length mirror Dr. Willard was pointing to. I envisioned myself standing there in the next six days. It was more than I could stand. Everyone in the room knew why I was crying and especially Becky. In just a few short days, my life would be different. I'd have to allow people to help me. I'd have to emotionally deal with surgery. I left with my packet of information, papers to read, and pain in my heart.

The trail was rocky and steep. I found myself slipping, grasping at anything I could to pull myself up. I didn't have time to stop and rest. I had to keep moving for time was of essence. The words "You won't look normal" played like a broken record through my mind. I finally found the courage to send Rosa a text asking her to whisper a prayer for me. I called Christy as I knew she would take my name before the throne. Neither of those women had a clue about my visit that day nor about the words I'd heard at the office. But I knew they would pray. At 2:30 p.m., a one-word text came to me—"Always." One word unspoken but taken to heart. I knew a prayer had been whispered to a holy God on my behalf.

God, I don't think I can do this! I guess I like trails and trials that are easy, even moderate, but O God, this is so hard. I look at my family and friends and wonder how this will change how they feel about me. Will they walk away from me? You alone know how I feel. Words. I've heard so many *of them today, yesterday, weeks ago. I'm not angry at You for allowing this to happen because You have a plan, but please help me. I want to bring honor to You. If one life is changed or one person is drawn closer to You, it will have been worth it all. I am struggling today. My tears are almost too much to handle. So God, help me and give me courage. That's all I know to ask for.*

Evening came. No one was really up for talking about my surgery. So the events of the day would stay closed up in my heart. I was amazed at how God worked. Once again, a text from Rosa came asking about my day. I responded, "Six days and my life will be changed forever." The text that came back was so profound: "Your body will no doubt, but your life will be richer."

Words have the power to do two things: bring death or bring life. Her text brought life. She had no idea of anything the doctor had told me, but I believe God had prompted her to write what she did. Proverbs 15:23 (NIV) says, "A person finds joy in giving an apt reply—and how good is a timely word." Talk about a timely word. I was learning that God was working through friendships to really bring scripture to life.

Father, I come to You at the end of a hectic day. I have tried to put pieces together, to make sense out of things, but it's too hard. Thank You for the tears for they cleanse my soul. You're good to me. You answered my closet prayer for a close friend. I have no words to describe how scared I am, but You already knew that. Just help me rest. Give me strength for another day. I do love You, Lord.

Not a restful night. I woke at 4:00 a.m. deep in thought. It was December 2, 2011, five days until surgery. I pondered in the wee hours of the morning all the words that had been spoken to me the previous day. I had choices to make—whether to accept or reject those words. I wanted to run and hide, but that wouldn't have helped. I decided to keep busy as there was much preparation for the next week.

While I was driving home after taking Jonathan to school, I thought, *Five days until surgery. Just five.* I couldn't explain it, but I knew God had spoken to me. Not audibly but to my heart. His presence was close. In the Bible, five is the number of grace; 2 Corinthians 12:9 (ESV) reads,

"But he said to me, 'My grace is sufficient for you, for my power is made perfect in weakness.'" He assured me He had all I needed to make it down my strenuous trail. I had already cried that day, but I was learning that tears did not always constitute weakness. I was learning God wants to use this strenuous hike in my life to bring honor to Him. I was determined to move forward and pray with intensity and passion for His will to be accomplished.

It's time to take a break on this trail. I don't know what I could have done differently in my life to have avoided this trail. Probably nothing. I pull out my trail map once more. Every trail has a name. In my haste, I see only the word *strenuous*. I look for the trail that was marked for me and came under the heading strenuous. I scan the trails' names. *Ahhh, here it is. Eagle Height Trail. A great name for a trail.* I believe I will rest here for a while before I move on. I look around and find a board with some writing on it. It's all about eagles. I am guessing this is probably on the trail to help others understand how the trail got its name. Since I'm resting here for the night, I figure a little reading will be good for me. And it just might shed some light on how strenuous this trail will become.

Eagles were designed to fly. It takes one to three months for them to build a nest. The male and female are committed to each other for life. They are great hunters, are rarely hunted, have excellent eyesight—up to one and a half miles—and live high up in trees. All these facts are interesting, but again, I don't know what this has to do with anything other than I might see eagles soaring while I'm hiking. I pull my Bible out of my backpack and open it to my marker at Isaiah 40:31 (ESV): "But they who wait for the LORD shall renew their strength; they shall mount up with wings as eagles; they shall run and not be weary, they shall walk and not faint." There it is in black and white. A verse pertaining to eagles. God must have something for me to learn while I am resting here. Could He be renewing my strength? Possibly, but I have to know more about mounting up with wings as eagles and waiting on the Lord.

I go back to the sign and try to find anything that might help me. Not a lot. So it'll be up to me to allow the Holy Spirit to speak to me regarding this verse.

God, here I am in a hard spot. The trail has become steeper, and I'm losing my footing more than I would like. There's not much to grasp hold of when I slip. You know I've fallen a few times. Here's this verse. You put it before me. Let me think on it and allow me to apply it to my life. Maybe it will help someone else who walks this trail in the future.

Sometime in the night, I awaken as has been the case for several weeks. The thought of eagles and renewing my strength is at the forefront of my thoughts. Hastily, I get my journal from my backpack and write.

> God designed eagles for soaring. The eagle floats with outstretched wings in the wind. It goes higher and higher and reaches heights unknown to other birds. It is never exhausted or weak from soaring. Eagles see the storm beforehand. They never flap their wings since that would cause them to struggle. Instead, they lock their wings, which enables them to be wind-aided. Amazingly, they fly on top of turbulent winds. Is it possible to soar over a trial? Is it possible for me to soar over the trial I am facing?
>
> Remember Job? God asked Job an interesting question in Job 39:27 (NIV): "Does the eagle soar at your command, and make its nest on high?" He was telling Job as He's telling me that He was in control of the animals, people, and the trials we face. To take flight, the eagle waits on a branch for the wind. Once hovering in the clouds, the eagle just soars on the winds to new heights. I need to rest on the strength of the Lord and allow the Holy Spirit to carry me above the trial. By doing so, He will renew my strength and allow me to mount up with wings as eagles.

I write faster as the thoughts race through my mind. "Renew my strength, Lord!" I cry out. The words flow from my pen like a racing river. I soar above my trials. Sounds peaceful, doesn't it? But how does it all happen? How do I get to the point of soaring and not sinking? The answer is found in Isaiah 40:31 (KJV): "But they who wait upon the LORD …"

Waiting is not easy for me especially when I'm going through a trial. What does the word *wait* mean in this verse? A little research reveals a big answer. Wait means two things in this verse. The first is obviously "to wait upon," but it has a second meaning—to "bind together (by twisting)" The Hebrew word is *qavah* (kaw-vaw).

How does that apply to me? To you? My waiting on God means willfully binding myself to His will and confidently expecting His plan to produce the best results. I am happy I brought my little journal and jot down some notes. Eagle Height Trail will continue to be steeper and more difficult in the days ahead. These are the thoughts that come to me as the day draws to a close: Eagles always have proper perspective. Their height when flying allows them to see all around. Eagles always have a purpose. God designed them for flying. For soaring. They welcome the wind. Eagle flights are peaceful. They don't worry about predators. Other birds cannot reach their heights.

Does God want me to have these three things in my life? A proper perspective on why I am on this strenuous trail, to know He has a purpose for all the words good and bad that have been spoken and all the tears that have silently streamed down my cheeks, and a purpose for me too? Could He really bring peace during such unsettledness and fear? If I want to mount up with wings as eagles on the trail, that will require that I pray intensely and passionately, read God's Word, fellowship with others, spend time with friends, and focus on Christ and what He is teaching me.

I wrote these words about eagles in my journal and placed it into my backpack. I am sure I will need to be reminded of this in the days ahead. It is still dark, and I return to my place of shelter to rest. I am amazed at how God has always known exactly what I've needed while on this trail. He has known when to use friends, emails, devotionals, and even texts. And now a lesson on eagles. He didn't allow me to know the name of the trail until today. I guess the trail had to reach a new height, a new level of difficulty before I could understand the importance of soaring like an eagle.

Dear Father, night has come, and time is ticking. The surgery is only four days away. Soaring like an eagle doesn't seem possible—not today anyway. I am thankful for the lesson, for knowing the trail's name, and for the rest You provided along the way. The darkness swallows me. Give me rest; the nights seem so long. My mind is always racing. I desperately need a healing touch. I just want to live my life for You and to be of service to others. Help me to wait for You.

I have stayed in this one spot for several days. As I gaze up the trail, I see the unforgiving terrain, the twists and turns that lie ahead. I don't know what to think. The trail has been relentless at times with steep hills, slippery rocks, and unforeseen bends in the path. I don't feel too much like an eagle today. The unknown is scary. I want to be like an eagle. God knows my heart, but taking the plunge to soar from the wind of His ways is tough.

Words. I come back to this thought often. I have received all kinds of words lately. Words that bring comfort, and words that bring condemnation. I try to remove myself from the hurtful and harmful words, but that isn't always easy. I need to move forward. I am thankful for the break, but if I want to soar with the eagles, I must press on.

Trail Marker 11
December 6, 2011

That was my last doctor's appointment before surgery. It was all so real. I couldn't believe that in less than eighteen hours I would undergo a double mastectomy. It was hard to say and hard to type.

I was thankful for Becky, Dr. Willard's surgical nurse, who gave me assurance she would be with me through the whole procedure. The doctor was very kind to me as he drew exactly where the cuts would be. He told me my procedure prior to surgery would be extremely painful. I had to go to nuclear medicine first thing and they would inject a needle in my left breast that would allow them to pinpoint the lymph node that fed into the pre-cancerous duct. That node would be removed and immediately tested for cancer.

I hadn't really moved from this location on the trail. My mind is reeling from all the words. Words, thousands of them, coming at me like fiery darts and scorching my already bruised heart. Words of death. Words of life. Powerful words.

I have tried multiple times today to pray, but my tears gush forth leaving the words I want to say hushed. I am thankful for those who are praying for me today. What else is there to say? I want to be healed. Completely. I know God knows my deepest thoughts and my every fear. He has brought me to this trail marker today to reveal Himself in a new way. The path is narrow, more so than before. The incline is steep. I slip and begin to fall. I lose my focus due to concentrating on words received that were not words of life. I am learning, slowly, how important words are for others. There are many days I wish I had learned this lesson earlier in life, but God's timing is always perfect.

God, You know how difficult today has been, a day full of words from doctors, nurses, family, and friends. You've heard and seen them all. I am so scared. I am lonely too. I just don't know if I can do what You are asking of me. I need You to look after Jonathan as he is hurting today. His fear has come alive in his heart. O God, be a father to him. Help him rely on You. I do love You. Help me find peace as the day moves forward. Guide the surgeons' hands in the morning. Give them rest tonight and wisdom in their decisions.

God, be with Rosa as she too is climbing this trail with me. Continue to speak to her. Allow her to rediscover who You are in her life. God, thank You for listening, for bottling up the tears that one day You will pour out because there are no tears in heaven.

Trail Marker 12
December 7, 2011

My day for surgery was my mothers' birthday. I needed to be at the hospital by 5:30 a.m. The unknown was a scary place. I knew that when the day was over, my life would be changed forever. I didn't know what to pray anymore except for His will to conquer my fear and accomplish His purpose.

I entered the operating room. Lots of things were going on. I had some trouble with the IV, so they decided they would work on it once I got to the operating room. I was so scared. One silent tear fell, and then another. A young woman put a mask over my nose and mouth. I thought I was choking, but then the words *Help me to rediscover You* come to my mind.

Those were the last words I remembered thinking before surgery began. It was still my prayer to rediscover God in my life in a more meaningful way.

I wasn't in the waiting room when the doctor came out, but according to Dr. Teppara, my life had been saved by doing a double mastectomy. No cancer in the lymph nodes. I knew God was listening to the cries of those who were waiting praying quietly in their hearts for God's will to be done.

I awakened at a place on my trail that I never thought I would reach. A place where the trails narrow path turned sharply and there was no place to turn back. I heard words from a familiar voice that was with me on this journey—not just ordinary words but prayerful words lifted up to a holy God on my behalf. Thank you, Phyllis.

Friends waited patiently for me to reach this part of the trail prayerfully considering what they personally wanted God to do in my life. And maybe considering what they wanted God to do in their lives. I rested and remembered the outpouring of love of friends and family—those who stayed for hours and those who held my hand.

Strange, the one thing I remember most was Rosa's holding my hand. I don't remember if she even spoke, but her touch made an impact on my life that day I will never forget. Her touch assured me that iron was sharpening iron at that moment; God was knitting our spirits together in a unique way.

My dear friend Christy brought her family to see me. Elliot, her husband, offered one of the most amazing prayers on my behalf. Michael, Beth, and Ashley were there with faces of love and cheer.

The human touch has more power to heal than we realize. There was something about the whole scene that revealed to me no matter what the outcome, my friends and family were there still climbing this trail alongside me. The path was narrow—not wide enough for two to walk side by side, so my dear friends came from behind and gave me the extra courage I needed to continue. Ecclesiastes 4:9–10 (NASB) says, "Two are better than one because they have a good return for their labor. For if either of them falls, the one will lift up his companion. But woe to the one who falls when there is not another to lift him up."

Trail Marker 13
December 8, 2011

If I could give this day a title, it would be "Words, Words, and More Words." I had more people giving me instructions on what to do when I got home—what I could and couldn't do. I was overwhelmed by words.

My loving husband, Brian, was taking care of Jonathan, so Rosa brought me home from the hospital and spoke gentle words to me. They were not words of instruction but words of compassion and love.

My parents were there to offer their support and take care of me. They had listened to the doctors' instructions and had followed us home. I didn't know where to begin thanking everyone for their willingness to help. A servant's heart was evident in each of them.

What am I supposed to be learning on this trail? Monument Mountain is hard at times to climb—especially this trail. I have learned that to climb a strenuous trail, I have to be in condition. I don't think God just throws us out onto a strenuous trail without first giving us some other trails and trials to train on. I reflect on my life and see where I had some easy and moderate trails and trials to endure but unfortunately didn't always finish strong. I complained, questioned, whined, and got angry without learning the wonderful lessons God was trying to teach me.

O God, I come to You trying to make sense of all that has just happened in my life. I feel so confused at times. My mind is going in so many directions. I want this to be just a really bad dream, but it is reality. My body has been changed forever. It is more than I can bear! I feel empty and so alone. No one hears my tears as they fall. No one sees them. They drop one by one and disappear. Please, dear Jesus, don't leave me here all alone. I am scared.

The trail has winded me. I was emotionally drained, and discouragement was finding its way into my heart. I finally had the strength to look at myself today. What a horrible sight! I sobbed. I did not think there were words to describe the emptiness I felt. I was so thankful my mother was there with me. Ever so gently, she rubbed my back and encouraged my troubled soul. There's nothing there except cuts, stitches, and four tubes hanging from my side. My sobbing doesn't stop.

God, I don't know what I need right now. I feel so lonely, like the world is moving ahead without me. I don't like it here. I hate what has happened to me. I cannot even believe it at times. I still hear those words—*cancer, surgery, double mastectomy.* God, how do I go forward? How do I stay strong when I feel so weak?

I find a nice rock to sit on and look at my surroundings. I see a sign posted and get up to take a closer look at the message. It tells me this part of the Eagle Height Trail is extremely stony. I figured as much. I had been having problems getting my footing since Trail Marker 10. The stones around me are all oddly shaped, so I put some in my backpack. I love rocks. They make great paperweights.

This is where I will rest. My emotions are getting the best of me. I will not allow myself to be fearful of any emotion; at one time in my life, they were revered as monsters. Instead, I will allow my feelings to filter through me and release the pain, hurt, loneliness, and discouragement in my soul.

This is a great place to rest. It has given me time to reflect on what has happened and assess my surroundings. According to what I read, this trail is stony, which means slippery, so getting my footing at times will be hard. I must be careful to make it to the next trail marker. I still cannot make a lot of sense out of all that has happened. I lie awake at night and wonder the question we all ask, *Why?* Silent tears come more frequently and give some relief to my weary soul. I guess I am glad no one hears or sees them. They are just between God and me, though I wish at times others would show some emotion. I have never been so full of emotions in my life. I have felt them all lately—hurt, sadness, guilt, loneliness, and pain. Pain emotionally, not so much physically. It just seems like one really bad dream. My life changed forever in a matter of weeks.

I don't have strength to move from where I am, but I must make an effort. Staying in one place too long is not good since it allows me to feel sorry for myself. This has been a good rest for me, a time to reflect and plan, but it's time to gather my things and press on.

The trail is extremely stony, and the terrain is hard to maneuver at times. I find myself falling back more than I make progress. Isn't that how it is in life? We move a few steps in the right direction and then setbacks occur. I am beyond exhaustion and want to get to the end of this trail. It's so narrow, and roots seem to spring up from the ground and grab at my feet making it all the harder to reach the top.

Soar like an eagle? Not today, Lord. I can't even think straight. Why have You brought me to this place? I feel numb. I cannot continue without Your help, Your strength, Your guidance. I just can't do it, Lord. I'm scared and lonely. I wish the loneliness would stop. Everyone is celebrating, shopping, and getting ready for Christmas. I just want to be well.

Trail Marker 14
December 21, 2011

The day was one of those days of the unknown. Fear swept over my soul as the place where they took out the tube on the left side started to swell. I called the doctor, and he told me to get there quickly. I did. My left breast was infected—*infection* was not the word I wanted to hear. They reopened the hole and drained as much infection as they could. I was to go back on December 23. I was on another round of antibiotics plus one to prevent pneumonia. I was praying for healing.

Setback, hindrance, delay, obstruction, obstacle—destructive words. A setback is defined as "something that reverses or delays the progress of somebody or something," The medicine made me sick to my stomach. I slept for fifteen hours on Thursday. I was feeling more exhausted as I tried to climb Eagle Height Trail. I didn't think I could go any farther.

Trail Marker 15
December 23, 2011

I met with Dr. Willard; he reopened the hole where the tube was and drained more infection. He also put an antibiotic in the tissue expander. He was so encouraging and kind.

Just when we were all thinking things were great, I receive a phone call about fifteen minutes after I had left the office. Bad news. The antibiotic he had used was on my allergy list, so I needed to get back there as quickly as I could. I turned the car around and went back. He drained the expander of the antibiotic and saline solution. Then he flushed out the expander with more saline and refilled it with saline, another antibiotic, and Benadryl. I was thankful Jonathan had his permit. He drove me home and did a great job.

So there I was again clinging to the word *setback*. Dr. Willard said, "Worst-case scenario, we take out the tissue expander. It's a minor setback. I just don't want you in the hospital over Christmas."

He asked me how Jonathan was handling things. "Everyone is at a different place," I said. I told him about his fear of my dying from an allergic reaction to medication. "He just wants a mom around." He spoke words of hope. "Tell him he'll have a mom around. You didn't experience full-blown cancer. It'll be okay." *Thank you, Dr. Willard* I said in my heart—a reminder that things could have been worse. Much worse.

Setback—my whole life seems to be one major setback right now. One second I feel great, and then there's the possibility of more surgery if this round of antibiotics doesn't work. If I could run and hide, I would—but then that spells defeat. Defeat is simply failure to win or realize a goal, and my goal is to finish this strenuous trail. Too many times in my life have I experienced defeat. And it is a painful and lonely experience.

This part of the trail has taken the wind out of my sails. The words this week have not been words of life. They have imparted pain and fear deep in my soul. My soul yearns for healing to come and for my body to be made whole. I am clinging to the words *no cancer*.

The trail is narrow, and I find a place beneath a rock overhang to park myself for a while. The words from Psalm 121:1–2 (ESV) are in the forefront of my mind: "I lift up my eyes to the hills, From where does my help come from? My help comes from the LORD, who made heaven and earth." The mountain trail is steep, but my help must come from God alone. I pull out my little black journal. I have much to write.

The hours pass slowly as I write about the loneliness, fear, and pain I feel. I have tried not to complain to anyone, to keep an upbeat attitude, but this setback has disheartened me so much. My prayer for tonight comes from Psalm 143:5–8, 10 (ESV)

God, I am so discouraged. I am lonely and scared, scared of so many things—medicines, rejection of people, surgery. You know all about that. So tonight, I pray Your words back to You, for it is here I will find comfort and strength in one of the darkest hours of my life.

> I remember the days of old; I meditate on all that You have done, I ponder the work of Your hands. I stretch out my hands to You; my soul thirsts for You like a parched land. Answer me quickly, O LORD! My spirit fails! Hide not Your face from me, lest I be like the ones who go down to the pit. Let me hear in the morning of Your steadfast love, for in You I trust. Make me know the way I should go, for to You I lift up my soul. Teach me to do Your will, for You are my God! Let Your good Spirit lead me on level ground.

So with that, God, I will rest my weary body. I will desperately seek You as I navigate this trail You have asked me take. Thank You for friends who pray. Thank You for friends who find words that are a healing balm for my broken spirit.

Today is Christmas. I feel empty as I am not able to participate in so many events. I feel hollow. Families are gathering and children are playing, and here I sit limited in all I can and would love to do. I promised myself I wouldn't allow myself to be in this dreadful place called discouragement. I go back to my prayer of "Answer me quickly, O LORD! My spirit fails!" I only want to feel good, to feel like doing something. I am sick and tired of sitting all day long. I want to scream. I try to look ahead and realize God is in control and has brought me this far. And with great reports—no cancer.

Don't think I'm ungrateful. I am more thankful than any word can express. I know a lot of my problems come from all the medications I am on, and I have never been one to take medications unless absolutely necessary. The one word that haunts me day and night is *setback*. We have all been there at some time. Maybe not through surgery but emotionally and even spiritually, but I know that setbacks are what we make them. I can choose to make this place of discouragement a place of permanent residence or find it to be only temporary and make plans to move forward.

O Father, where do I begin? It has been a day of silent tears, a day of just needing to feel Your closeness. It is Christmas. I pray You would come to me at a time I need You most. I want to be like the shepherds when the angel of the Lord appeared to them. I want to hear the words *Do not be afraid.* I want to be open to follow Your plan whatever it may be.

Let me be thankful for the pain, for friends, for family, and for healing. As I sit here alone, let me feel Your presence as I have never felt it before. O God, let me rediscover You in a new, fresh way. Help me see this setback as something that will honor You one day. Please don't let me see this as an annoyance, for then, Father, I would surely lose my way.

A new day has dawned, and I am anticipating that God will do great things in my life today. I went to bed last night around 7:30 p.m. just to be alone and spend time with my heavenly Father. Oh how those silent tears fell to my pillow, and how the words *Lord, have mercy* escaped my mouth between sobs. My prayer last night was simple: "Make Yourself known to me." I just kept praying, actually begging God to make Himself known to me. It happened. I felt a peace come over me like never before as if He were covering me with a blanket of peace. And then I slept. So today, I am giving Him thanks for the peace that covered me and kept me through the night.

Trail Marker 16
December 28, 2011

Another doctor appointment at 4:30 p.m. with Dr. Willard. It wasn't so bad. The culture they had taken had not grown anything, so we were still in the guessing game about antibiotics. He said that the redness looked better but that he might have to remove the tissue expander. "It's only a minor setback," he said. I was to make another appointment for Friday.

I am comfortable here on this part of the trail, but I must move on. I am looking at some awesome scenery. The eagles are flying high above me, which reminds me that I too want to soar on wings as eagles. I feel I've fallen into the trenches of despair, the very place I don't want to be. I am worried about my body not fighting this infection and losing the tissue expander. I pack up and move forward. Each step is harder than the previous one. I finally find another spot to rest my weary body and plop down. Will this ever end?

Trail Marker 17
December 30, 2011

Dr. Willard saw a little improvement but not enough to satisfy him. "You're not out of the woods yet," he said. "The redness looks much better, but the culture still has not grown anything, so we're still guessing about antibiotics. Just remember that if we have to take out the tissue expander, it's only a setback, not a disaster."

We talked about Duke basketball though neither of us was a fan. We joked around, and I made another appointment for Thursday, January 5.

The hike to the next trail marker will not be easy. I find a place to stop for the night and reflect. I have been thinking about the word *faith* since about 3:30 a.m. What is faith? Do I have the faith I need to get through this? This has been a very lonely week for me. I see Brian struggling to know what he can do for me and even what to say. I have tried to talk to him about the surgery and the healing process. It's more than any of us can bear, and I'll not judge him for what he cannot verbalize in this moment. I constantly wonder what he is thinking and feeling. In his time and his kind way, he will share. Now is not the time to pronounce judgment on how others should feel when I don't even know how I feel myself.

According to Hebrews 11:1 (NASV), faith is "the assurance of things hoped for, the conviction of things not seen." My faith is being tested while hiking this strenuous trail. I cannot see God, but I have a strong belief that He is with me. Is that faith? I cannot audibly hear Him speak to me, but He uses the Word and the words of others to comfort and encourage me. Is that faith? How hard is it to get faith? How hard is it to keep faith?

My thoughts race as I continue my quest for understanding. Matthew 17:20 (NASV) reads, "If you have the faith the size of a mustard seed, you will say to this mountain, 'Move from here to there,' and it will move; and nothing will be impossible to you." Have you seen a mustard seed? It's so tiny. So as I sit by the crackling fire, I ask myself, *Is this all God requires of me to start growing my faith?* It is obvious to me for the first time in my life that God isn't asking me to start with something bigger than I am able to give. Romans 12:3 (NASB) says, "God has allotted to each a measure of faith." Faith equals my full surrender to God's will, so asking God to heal me must be in accordance with His will, not mine.

Monument Mountain is gigantic. If I have faith, does that mean God will allow me to tell this mountain to move? Not exactly. I have had plenty of time to camp out at Trail Marker 17. I've been asking myself, *What is my mountain that seems insurmountable, impossible, and intimidating?* My personal mountain represents several things—fear, being rejected, losing my family, losing friends, not being able to finish the hike, and most of all, an overwhelming sense of being left alone.

We all have personal mountains in our lives; it just takes courage to acknowledge they're there. I look up to what seems to be a mountain so gigantic that only God could move it. That's it! I could never move the personal mountains in my own life, but planting the small mustard seed of faith in my heart will allow my faith to grow thus producing faith fruit. I produce faith fruit when I believe and know in the deepest part of my soul that God is trustworthy and to be praised above everything. Mountain moving belongs to God, who in return teaches me through the mountains in my life not to be fearful when facing a difficult situation because He is the true mountain mover. A Bill Hybels quote I learned a while back is, "Look less at the mountain and more at the mountain mover."

Monument Mountain is progressing trail marker by trail marker. I don't always see the good hand of God guiding me along the narrow path. My feet have stumbled. Setbacks have occurred. But I go back to Dr. Willard's words, "It's only a setback, not a disaster." So I will rest here a while longer and ponder the faith fruit that will become part of my life.

God, I need a mustard-seed faith to be produced in my life especially if I am going to make it to the next trail marker. You are the great mountain mover, and only You can move the mountain of fear, pain, loneliness, and despair I feel. I am clinging to Your Word for guidance. You will not fail me. It has been a week of many challenges, but let me be like the psalmist and say, "I will bless the LORD at all times, his praise shall continually be in my mouth" (Psalm 34:3 ESV). I want to praise You, rediscover You, and serve You with my whole heart. All I ask for this day is strength and to remember setbacks are not permanent. Disasters are things that cause serious loss and destruction, so I ask for understanding of this setback.

Please God, tell me what I am supposed to be learning. I can't sleep and can barely eat. My soul longs to know You intimately so I can become the servant You need me to be. Bless my friend Rosa as she spends time with her family. I am glad she is part of my family and You are giving her strength to hike alongside me. Give her safety as she is in Puerto Rico and in sweet fellowship with those she loves so much. Grow her in her faith. I'm so glad You didn't require either of us to start with something bigger than a mustard seed. I love You, Lord, more each day.

Wow! I can't believe I'm starting the new year on Monument Mountain. I've been here for two months. I thought this ordeal would be over long before now. The trail becomes more difficult with each step. When will this end? I am thankful for my journal and the power of the pen.

January 1, 2012

The start of a new year. I wonder what it has in store for me. It has been a difficult day as the infection doesn't seem to improve, and now, I have something that resembles shingles. So more medicines and another antibiotic added to the one I'm taking. I am desperately fighting discouragement. I have tried to talk with Brian today, but he is silent. I know he too is at a loss for words. We all process things in our own way and in our own time, so I cannot expect my family to rush the emotions they feel; that wouldn't be healthy. In the midst of sadness, I can always count on a little humor from Jonathan. He told me, "We prayed for you over dinner when you were in the hospital." How funny. I was blessed with pizza, but I'm sure they lifted their prayers on my behalf in their private times with God.

The medicine, infections, and loneliness seemed to run amuck through every emotional nerve I have. I was so angered and hurt. I never asked anyone else to walk in my shoes—just to walk alongside me. I was struggling for answers on this first day of a new year.

I have wondered so many times why God is allowing me to suffer. Some believe God is chastising me. They even called to ask me if I felt this was what God was doing in my life. Wow! It amazes me how judgmental people can be. I have given this a lot of thought lately. I don't believe God is chastising me. I believe my situation will be used in some way to bring others closer to the Lord, myself included. Job 2:13 (NASB) reads, "Then they sat down on the ground with him for seven days and seven nights with no one speaking a word to him, for they saw that his pain was very great." All Job needed was companionship and comfort. The silence they offered Job was a language understood by the heart of friends. At times, friends do more good when they are silent than when they speak. Job's friends should have remembered their actions a few chapters later when they started giving opinions as to why Job was suffering. Having people make judgment calls about my situation has hurt me deeply; I just don't understand why Christians act the way they do.

I have been pondering the issue of suffering. No, I don't like it, don't enjoy it, and don't want to be here. I have cried out to God for healing, rest, and comfort. Silent tears have flowed from the remote parts of my heart, those hidden places where pain, fear, hurt, and grief reside. Will God rescue me? What is His reasoning behind the suffering and pain? The only place I know to find comfort is in the Word. Deuteronomy 29:29 (ESV) states, "The secret things belong to the LORD our God, but the things that are revealed belong to us and to our children forever, that we may do all the words of this law." This tells me that there are things in life He has determined not to make plain. God has secrets, so there will always be unanswered questions. I am learning I may never know why I have had to suffer, but believers suffer for various reasons, two of which I am looking at intently.

Believers can suffer. In 1 Peter 1:6 (NASB), we are assured of trials: "In this you greatly rejoice, even though now for a little while, if necessary, you have been distressed by various trials." That one hopeful phrase—"for a little while"—tells me trials don't last forever but serve a purpose. I believe one purpose of my suffering is so I can help others in their times of trouble. We are called to "bear one another's burdens" in Galatians 6:2 (ESV). Burdens connote extra-heavy loads—our difficulties and pains—so we are to help each other in such times.

One day, I will be able to bring comfort to others when they are hiking a strenuous trail; 2 Corinthians 1:4 (NIV) says it best: "Who comforts us in our troubles, so that we can comfort those who are in any trouble with the comfort we ourselves are receive from God." Something to write in your journal, friends—God comforts me. God comforts you.

The second reason I think God is allowing me to go on this strenuous hike is to reveal what I really love. When illness and death knock at your door, it clarifies things in a way nothing else can. I go back to the song "Let Me Rediscover You" and have found throughout this strenuous hike that I am finding out who God really is in my life. He is not the God I thought I knew. Deuteronomy 13:3b (NIV) reads, "The LORD your God is testing you to find out if you love the LORD your God with all your heart and with all your soul." I went on a little search in the thesaurus for the word *all* to give me a mental picture of what God means by this word. Here's what the thesaurus had to say: "All: completely, entirely, wholly, totally, everything, unreservedly, and exclusively."

I am pondering this thought. Do I love the Lord exclusively? Or are other things calling my name to attract my love? I know God calls us to love our families and friends, but the world also calls us to love the things in it. Do we show more affection and love to the world than to the Word? Testing and trials will always be around. Believers are not exempt from testing, but their tests will be for a little while to find out what they really love. My passion is to rediscover God daily in a new and fresh way.

O Father, You know my heart. I have no words to pray except that I need You. My heart is so heavy, and my tears drown the words I would pray. I need You, Father. Oh how I need You.

Today is January 4, 2012. I am still sitting here at Trail Marker 17. I'll hang out here the rest of the day and start moving tomorrow. I have been here for several days thinking about so many things—about my personal faith in God, my suffering, and my testing. It has been a hard time. I don't recall God ever promising me this trail would be easy. I recall the word *strenuous* was revealed, and strenuous it has been. My tears have flowed out as rivers of ink allowing the penning of this journey to be possible—silent tears writing about the hike of a lifetime.

I found these words to an old hymn by Eugene Clark. I don't know the tune, but the words speak to me.

I do not know what lies ahead
The way I cannot see
But One stands near to be my guide
And He will show the way to me.
I know who holds the future
And He guides me with His hand
With God things don't just happen
Everything by Him is planned.

It was some hike up to Trail Marker 18. A lot of twists and turns, but I have made it. It's a different kind of place—nothing like all the other stops I've made. I throw my backpack to the dusty ground. I am in no frame of mind to continue the trail up Monument Mountain. I thought I was almost there, but the word *setback* has been my enemy of late. My mind is whirling, and discouragement is washing over me.

Trail Marker 18
January 5, 2012

I had an appointment with Dr. Willard to see if the left breast area had improved since I had been taking all these antibiotics. I'd dreaded this appointment for days because the redness was still there.

I sat in the room waiting for Dr. Willard. One look on his face and I knew I'd lose the tissue expander. There was no laughter, no joking around, just serious talk. "This is not the end of the world," he said gently. All I could do was nod. If I had spoken a word, my tears would have gushed out. They were already flooding my soul. He said, "Whatever path God takes us on, that's how we'll go. You'll be just fine." So on Tuesday January 10, 2012, the tissue expander would be removed. Unless God performed a miracle.

As soon as I got in my car, I broke down in tears. It was more than I could handle. I receive a text from Rosa during my breakdown: "There with you." I sent a message telling her the news. She texted again, "Can u talk now?" She called when she was in Puerto Rico. I could barely speak, but her voice and words assured me she was still hiking alongside me on this strenuous trail. I was struggling with all this. I didn't feel like I had much fight left in me. I had cried myself to sleep the previous night. Oh how I cried. Life is cruel. All I want is to be well, to move on with my life, but God has put me on the path, and in the doctor's words, "That's how we'll go."

God, I can't do this. I can't go through more surgery. I feel all alone. You know that. How many more tears do I have to shed? I just can't do it anymore. I have nothing left in me to fight. I look in the mirror and am horrified. Every day, I am forced to look at how my body has changed. It is hard for me to look at myself. I feel alienated in my own home. I sit alone, eat alone, and sleep alone. I'm tired of sleeping straight up in a chair. I'm tired of looking at four walls while everyone is at work or school. I don't know what to do. I call out to You so many times, but things don't appear to be changing. But maybe they are. And now this surgery on Tuesday. God, please heal me before then. I know it is not out of Your power to do so. I can't continue to do this alone. I just can't.

The tears drop one by one scalding my face. I can't stop them, but then again, no one is here to see them anyway. The news of more surgery is overwhelming. It will be a long night here on Trail Marker 18. I struggle to find a place to sit as the rocks are jagged and the roots stick out of the ground. Maybe this trail marker is made to make the hiker uncomfortable. I shove myself between some rocks and lean against my backpack. It's time to think about plan B as Dr. Willard calls it.

I look around at the rocks and roots that have slowed my progress. My eyes catch a rock nearby with some letters carved in it. I pull myself up slowly and carefully inch my way to the rock. I brush some of the dust and dirt away and read, "Baca," "ps," and "84." I don't get it. I maneuver my way back to where I was sitting and ponder the letters and numbers. Baca means nothing to me. And *ps 84* could mean whoever wrote it was reminding the reader, "Hey, don't forget this happened in 1984." This has me intrigued.

I gaze to the heavens. The stars are popping out. The sky looks like it has glitter sprinkled across it. I prop up on my backpack and think about the message etched on the stone. Then it hits me. It's not the ps one would write at the bottom of a letter. No, it's the abbreviation for the word *psalm*—it means Psalm 84. I quickly pull out my Bible and find Psalm

84. I am hoping this will give me insight about this hike. I read verse 6 (NASB): "As they go through the Valley of Baca they make it a place of springs."

The stars give off radiant light as I look for the meaning of the word *Baca*. I know it's a valley, but I wonder what purpose it served. I searched throughout the night until I found my answer. The Valley of Baca is a literal place—possibly in Palestine. The Valley of Baca was regarded as a place of darkness and tears, thus the Valley of Baca is the Valley of Tears or the Valley of Weeping. It was a treacherous and gloomy place, but one had to pass through it to get to the place of worship—Zion.

It all makes sense. I am in my personal Valley of Weeping. I am trying to make it to the top of Monument Mountain, but first, I must go through a time of weeping. At times, the way has been treacherous. The silent tears that have become my song in the night have purpose; they are leading me to a place of refreshment, a place of springs.

Though my eyes are drowned in tears, my heart filled with pain and sorrow, God, through the psalmist, is assuring me there are sweet refreshments in the Valley of Tears. What kind of refreshments I do not know.

I still have not pieced this entire puzzle together. Why did Trail Marker 18 reveal this to me? Will there be more hardships ahead? More surgery? Or will God perform a miracle before January 10? What am I supposed to learn here? I realize I am truly in the Valley of Weeping. I rest my head on my backpack and let the tears fall until I find sleep.

I awake still thinking about Psalm 84. I gather my things and make my way up the trail. I must try to reach the next destination, but I don't feel so good today. I press forward until I cannot go any farther. I collapse and find I have reached Trail Marker 19.

Trail Marker 19
January 6, 2012

My left breast was draining infection. I made a quick phone call to Dr. Willard thinking that was good news. But I was told it revealed only one thing: "The tissue expander has to come out today." Why hadn't God performed a miracle? How much longer would I have to travel through this Valley of Tears?

I made it to his office with much fear. I was so saddened by the news, but it had to be done. Dr. Willard and his nurse, Becky, had done their best to make a terrible situation tolerable. Since I hadn't been put to sleep, he was able to talk to me throughout the procedure and tell me what was happening. He took the expander out, stitched me up, and put in a drain tube. I know he hated that as much as I did, but my body couldn't fight the infection. I didn't know if I could keep on fighting. Sometimes, I was feeling my ability to fight was slipping away.

I sat up and waited for further instructions. Everyone in the office was supportive and empathetic about what I had just experienced. Judy came back, and I shared about my journaling, about how writing had gotten me through so much of what I had experienced. I shared with them how I viewed this as a strenuous hike God had given me. Judy hugged me and said, "You've got some mighty good hiking shoes."

I had never thought about that angle of it. Hiking shoes were such an important commodity when maneuvering through tough terrain. I'd have to give that concept some more thought. Becky—who could have asked for a better nurse?—assured me I would be okay and said, "Though you didn't have to have chemo or radiation, you still have the same emotions. You lost both breasts, and most people don't understand how emotional that can be." She was right. I was grateful I didn't have to experience chemo or radiation, but I had still experienced a loss.

I drove home. My mother was sitting on the passenger side. She was so supportive, so full of love, so filled with a mother's compassion. I was amazed at her strength. I knew she hurt for me and didn't understand this either. I was glad it was over and no one had to worry with this on Tuesday. I didn't want to be a burden to anyone. I felt empty. I had wanted a miracle—all the infection to be gone and to be well on my way to a speedy recovery. But another setback; six weeks and another surgery to replace the tissue expander.

Well, God, here I am again crying and begging You to intervene. You gave me a sign using Psalm 84 on Trail Marker 18. You knew I would be in the Valley of Tears today. How much longer before I find it to be a place of springs? Are the desires of my heart wrong because I want to be healed? I'm not worth much to anyone at this point in my life. It seems my family has deserted me, ran away. I know that's not true, but it's how I feel. I am overcome in my soul with grief. God, I know You are here, but where? Why didn't You just heal me? Why do I have to face more surgery? What strength I had is failing. Please help me. I don't know what else to pray.

Sleep is nowhere to be found. I am in a lot of pain. Emotionally, I am a wreck, and here I am lying alone to face the night. Tears have become my song in the night as they lull me in and out of sleep—a restless lullaby. In my mind, I keep telling myself to hang on, keep fighting, but I can't. This is a bigger battle than I had bargained for. It's not a one-person fight. I know in my heart God is with me, but I need something tangible. I usually find myself stronger, but not today. I feel like the very life has been sucked out of me. I feel like a loser. The restless lullaby plays louder in my heart. I can't shut the tears off. Who cares anyway? I am alone, so no one knows the difference. God, how many more silent tears will fall before those I love hear them?

A restless night. But moving from here is a must. I cannot hunker down in the Valley of Baca; it is much too emotional. There must be something better ahead of me, and I intend to find it. I have to leave the trail marker. I am trying to sort things out. Maybe suffering allows us to sort things out. My fear has risen along with my other emotions. The longer I sit here, the worse I feel, so today, I will begin the tedious climb to Trail Marker 20.

Trail Marker 20
January 11, 2012

I had an appointment with Dr. Willard. I really wanted to get this tube taken out, but sad to say, it would be with me another couple of days. He seemed to be encouraged that the redness was dissipating. Still red, which meant infection was lurking in my body. I am happy, but I wished Friday had never happened. I wished none of this had happened. I was to return on Friday, January 13, 2012, for another appointment and hopefully the removal of the drainage tube.

So there I was again waiting for answers. Waiting to see if the infection would leave my body or if there would be another change in medication. Waiting was so hard. I was finding that nights brought a perspective that would not occur during the day. In the darkest hours of the night, I found myself reviewing the past three months in great detail. The blanket of darkness provided a secure place for me to let down my guard and weep. I had done a lot of weeping at night because so few people understood the emotions that came with having both breasts removed. During the day, I felt I had to be strong, a survivor, but the night offered me what daylight could not—perspective—that God often turned to peace.

The hour is late. I will stop here for the next couple of days before I move on to the next trail marker. I have much to think about especially the surgery coming up in February. I do not want my body to reject this next tissue expander. My mind is constantly thinking, which rarely allows for a good night's rest. I have much on my mind after my doctor's visit today, questions I wanted to ask but didn't. I am so glad Becky, Dr. Willard's surgical nurse, works in that office. I wonder if she knows how much good she does the people she comes in contact with daily. I am blessed to know the office staff and especially Peggy, who greets me as I sign in each time. That initial contact often calms my fears. I am thankful for all of them because of their genuine concern for my well-being.

Trail Marker 21 is just ahead. I wonder what the hike there will be like. I would say that today, January 12, 2012, has been a heavy day—it has had its share of hardships and disappointments. For the first time, I feel not just about my situation but also the way things are in my home, my life. It's hard to explain without appearing judgmental or acting as the accuser, but I am hurt, angry, disappointed. A lot of words come when one can't change a situation, when one can't fix a problem, when one is at a crossroads. I'm sure what I want from those around me, but I cannot ask them to stop living their lives while I make sense out of mine.

I like to fix things, make things right, find solutions, but today, I cannot find a solution for the brokenness I feel. I can't seem to right what has gone wrong in my life. In my body. I find myself in a constant search for an answer to the question why. So many things are happening around me, but I cannot fix them either. Fear, family, friends, rejection, loneliness, pain, sorrow, and grief have been damaged or are causing me damage along this strenuous trail. Obviously, crying doesn't fix things or this whole thing would be over, but silent tears serve a purpose—they relieve some of the pressure in my heart. But not all of it.

Tomorrow, I will make my way to the next trail marker. I don't think the way will be easy as I observe heights I have never climbed looming in front of me. I haven't been able to right the wrong or make sense of anything that has happened in the past months. There are countless twists and turns in the trail ahead, and my fight is being interrupted by my fears. Discouragement is lurking in my soul and trying to stop me in my tracks. There are no alternate routes to the top of Monument Mountain, so I will have to press on or give up.

Where do I begin, God? I can't fix what has gone wrong in my body or in my home. Before all this, things were very different. I don't expect anyone to really understand, but I need someone. I'm tired of being alone. I know You are here, but something tangible would be so nice right now. A hand to hold, a hug, a conversation. Today has been so hard—emotions running wild, words without purpose being launched, problems without solutions. I still don't know why I'm on this trail. I haven't forgotten You. I really need You to intervene on my behalf. Without hope, there will be no healing. You know what I need before I ask for it. Please provide me what You deem sufficient for this hour, this day, and get me safely to the next trail marker.

I have put on my hiking shoes and slung my backpack over my shoulder. I am headed to Trail Marker 21. What seems like a short distance really isn't, but I am here and waiting to see what I am to learn.

Trail Marker 21
January 13, 2012

I had an appointment with Dr. Willard to see if the drainage tube would be removed. It wasn't to be that day. "It's better to leave the tube in than to remove it too early." I asked, "Do you really see improvement?" He assured me he saw improvement. I was happy that the redness looked better to him. I would continue the antibiotics until I saw him again on Monday.

Maybe I didn't get the tube taken out, but I got something I needed much more—one-on-one time with Becky. It was nice to have someone who understood me and could answer so many of my questions. I could have cried a river that day, but I refrained from that. It was hard to stay strong in the midst of difficulties. I had many things to think about, to organize in my brain.

There is plenty of time to reflect here today since I don't plan to move on for another day. The night was long; my mind was in overdrive. The hike between trail markers was tiresome, and I reflect on the unforeseen terrain. Many setbacks have hindered my reaching the top of Monument Mountain, but it seems there's always a place of refuge when I come to another trail marker—a place to sit, rest, journal, and pray. Though I am physically alone, I feel God's presence as a reminder that He will not forsake me on my strenuous hike.

My thoughts go back to a statement made a week ago: "You've got some mighty good hiking shoes." I ponder shoes today and how shoes have affected my ability to climb a mountain such as this. So what makes hiking shoes so different from my other shoes? I think of four things that have allowed me to make it thus far on this trail. They help me realize several aspects of this hike I have not thought of previously.

How to Choose Hiking Shoes for Strenuous Trails and Trials in Life

- Find a shoe that fits your foot shape. Everyone's feet are shaped differently, so finding the right shoe is not as simple as asking your friends what shoes work for them.

  We will all be asked to hike various trails in life. Some will be easy, while others will be strenuous. God does not give each of us the same burden to carry; thus, the shoes I am wearing today would not be the same for someone on an easy trail. I can get advice from my friends, but that's all. My calling is to find the pair of shoes that will enable me to climb the trail I have been called to. The shoes my friends are wearing are different since they choose to walk with me but are not experiencing the extensiveness of the hike. They don't tire as easily, are not agitated as quickly, and have more endurance, which is why God has given me a specific friend for this journey. Proverbs 12:25 (NASB) says, "Anxiety in a man's heart weighs it down, But **a good word makes it glad**" (emphasis mine).

- The lighter the weight the better. The heavier the shoes, the harder you will have to work to lift your feet with every step. Okay, so we all have personal baggage we tote from place to place. I'm sure that if I look in my backpack I'd find unnecessary things I have carried with me including anger, an unforgiving spirit, hurt, discouragement, resentment, fear of rejection, pain, grief, sorrow, loneliness, and fear. Some of these things are necessary in the healing process, but they cannot become a crutch for me to hobble on through my hike.

  Lightweight shoes will enable me to have additional freedom. I am challenging myself to go through my backpack and see what hindering baggage I have. Hebrews 12:1 (ESV) reads, "Let us lay aside every weight, and sin which clings so closely, and let us run with endurance the race that is set before us." What baggage are you carrying that hinders your walk with God? Identify it and get rid of it. I know my hike will not be as burdensome if I leave some of my baggage here.

- Buy one size larger than normal—a larger shoe gives your feet room to grow. My hiking shoes are allowing me to grow. Of course not physically but spiritually. This trail/trial has certainly been strenuous, but growth has occurred. Though there have been many days of discouragement and setbacks, I find myself asking God to help me rediscover Him in a fresh, new way. We are all capable of stunting our growth by not listening to God or becoming so discouraged that we dare not budge from the place God has put us. The harder the trail/trial, the more endurance He gives. Look at what Paul says in Romans 5:3–5 (ESV).

  More than that we rejoice in our sufferings, knowing that **suffering produces endurance**, and **endurance produces character**, and **character produces hope**, and hope does not put us to shame, because God's love has been poured out into our hearts through the Holy Spirit who has been given to us. (Emphasis mine)

- Traction is a very important part of a hiking shoe; good traction helps you not lose your balance. Traction gives you stability and helps you not slip too far back when you meet resistance—roots, fallen limbs, wet rocks, or leaves.

  Traction on this trail has come from God's Word—the only way I have been able to move from one trail marker to the next. When the terrain on the trail changed, I found myself in the trenches of despair, but the Word gave me strength to move forward. Just when I thought I was moving forward, I found myself not advancing at all. Silent tears filled my heart, and I thought about giving up, but God spoke to me through friends and family to give me extra traction with their encouraging words.

God's Word is full of traction verses, and Psalm 119 contains many that give me stability when hiking unknown and strenuous trails. Here are a few.

- Psalm 119:15–16 (ESV): "I will meditate on your precepts and fix my eyes on your ways. I will delight in your statues; I will not forget your word."
- Psalm 119:24 (ESV): "Your testimonies are my delight; they are my counselors."
- Psalm 119:50 (ESV): "This is my comfort in my affliction, that your promise gives me life."
- Psalm 119:71–72 (ESV): "It is good for me that I was afflicted, that I might learn your statues. The law of your mouth is better to me than thousands of gold and silver pieces."
- Psalm 119:114 (ESV): "You are my hiding place and my shield; I hope in your word."

I have learned much about hiking shoes over these past couple of days. I am packed and ready to head to the next trail marker. I am still assessing the articles in my backpack for I know I have to leave behind much of my baggage. I don't know why I find it so hard to leave such things behind. I don't need anything to make the hike more cumbersome.

God, I come to You because I cannot clean out my backpack by myself. I don't understand why I want to hold onto things that hinder my progress. I don't have a lot of time before I move to the next trail marker. If I can't free myself of this extra baggage, the way will be harder, and the way has already been tougher than I had anticipated. O God, I am looking at the stuff in my backpack. I can't do this alone. And alone is how I feel. Loneliness creeps alongside me on this trail. It is real, and it has overshadowed me many a night. My silent tears have been the result of my loneliness. I ask You to help me find a way to liberate myself from the extra things I carry. Especially loneliness.

I am headed to the next trail marker. There's no noise except my feet crunching on the dry leaves along the path. I have plenty of time to think, reflect, and wonder about the next place I will be asked to go. Will it be as difficult as it has been? Will there be any good news? I trudge forward. The path consists of small things—twigs, limbs, rocks protruding out of the ground that make it seem almost impassable at times. But I must keep moving. You see, I never did dump my extra baggage. My load is heavier than it should be. I don't know why I didn't just leave this mess behind.

Trail Marker 22
January 16, 2012

I had an appointment with Dr. Willard to see if the drainage tube could be removed. He was pleased with my progress, and the tube was removed. Stitches would come out on Wednesday. I had many questions, and he graciously answered them. The shocker of the day was when we were talking about the upcoming surgery to replace the tissue expander. I'd go home with another drain tube with a bulb. They even gave me back the bra I had turned in since mastectomy bras were hard to come by. That was strange. But the biggest shocker was when Dr. Willard said, "We'll start filling up that other tissue expander on Wednesday." I was taken by surprise. "I'll be lopsided," I said. But Becky said, "We'll give you something to stuff that bra with, something like pillow stuffing or shoulder pads," half-laughing with her award-winning smile.

I guessed the humor of it all was how you looked at it lopsidedness and all. I hadn't planned on getting the bra back, so that was kinda funny in a—um—lopsided way. The infection was getting better, which told us the antibiotic was working.

I enjoyed my visit because of the encouraging signs Dr. Willard was seeing. That gave me a ray of hope, something I hadn't had in a long time. Hope is a good four-letter word.

I couldn't wait to tell everyone all the stuff that had happened that day. Prior to my doctor's appointment, I'd had lunch with friends, and that was special. The unselfishness of my friends, family, and neighbors even for a brief time was iron sharpening iron. After our goodbyes, my friend gave me a gentle hug and said, "Let me know how the appointment goes." Her words were genuine, and that was important. I had so many silent fears that had led to silent tears. Fears no one knew about. Fears that lurked in the darkness of the night.

She called me later, and I told her I was no longer on house arrest. I told my parents the good news, and my mom said, "God is able, and He's faithful." I felt hope returning. We all had some good laughs about my appointment, and we were all more hopeful than we had been in a long time.

God, thank You for a friend who genuinely cares about me and takes time out of her busy schedule to visit me. I've felt so disconnected from everyone lately. I pray and pray, but loneliness and fear make their way into my heart. Please bless Rosa and my precious mom in a very special way for having servants' hearts, and be with the staff in Dr. Willard's office. Hope—please let this word sustain and follow me on my journey. I really love You!

The trek to Trail Marker 22 was tedious and at times treacherous. For a time, loneliness and fear walked beside me. I tried to ignore them, but I wasn't always successful. I will stay here for a day. I don't know how many more trail markers I will have to get to before the hike up Monument Mountain is complete. I feel safe here for the night. The stars are shimmering, and I feel at peace as I look at the heavens. Before I shut my eyes, I am once again reminded, "My help comes from the LORD, who made the heaven and earth" (Psalm 121:2 ESV). Fear and loneliness were my companions today. But peace has put them to rest for the night.

I can't say I had a restful night. My mind wouldn't shut off. My sleep was intermittent with thoughts about this hike and what lay ahead. It was a beautiful sight to see—the sun rising over the trees this morning. The radiant rays give me a sense of hope. Today, I will rest and get ready for the hike to Trail Marker 23. The climb continues to get steeper. I desire to be teachable at each place I rest and not grow weary with what God is doing in my life though I don't understand any of it.

I have been walking around this area all day. It's funny the things I've seen piled up in different areas. Not trash, but rocks with words on them—*fear*, *despair*, *impatience*, *stealing*, *lying*, *cheating*, *pain*, and *grief* are on a few of the rocks I have read since I discovered them a few hours ago. I wonder why people left them here.

I have another night here before I head out. I scrounge around reading the words on the rocks and discover a poster on the tree with Philippians 3:13 (ESV) on it. I pull out my Bible and read, "But this one thing I do; forgetting what lies behind and straining forward to what lies ahead."

I know I am to leave whatever hinders me at this place. I remember the stones I picked up at Trail Marker 13. I frantically dig through my backpack and find the stones. *What's hindering me right now?* I wonder about the other hikers who left stones behind. *Were they like me? Did they finish or turn back?* What I know is that I have weights in my backpack. I read some more rocks—a lot of baggage left behind—but did these hikers finish strong after releasing the extra weight? I wish I knew.

I find a comfortable spot and assess what is weighing me down. I go through my bag very carefully. What does God want me to get rid of to forget what is behind me and move forward to what lies ahead? I scribble the word *fear* on a rock. What are the things I am fearful of? More bad news. Losing friends. Not finishing strong. I toss my rock among the many there. I believe this rock is weightier than most of us think. Fear can tear at our minds until we become paralyzed.

I can't say I feel anything at the moment. I know fear was one of the most significant things weighing me down. Did other hikers feel a sense of joy or peace when they tossed their rocks on the pile? There has to be something more to this whole thing. Maybe I should go back, pick up my rock, and forget the whole matter. I came this far carrying that weight. I return to the pile of rocks, find mine, and shove it into my backpack. Who cares? I get up angry at the lack of explanation regarding the rocks but see a piece of paper flapping in the breeze. There are only two words on the paper: *Replacement Rocks.*

All I see is a pile of wordless rocks smoother and lighter than those I have in my bag, not much good for paperweights. I shuffle back to where I was sitting and try to make sense of the scenario. First, I find the pile of rocks with words on them. Next, I locate a verse from Philippians. Then I scribble what I feel is weighing me down and chuck it onto the pile. Yet I feel no different. Shortly afterward, I spot the paper with two words written on it and find smooth, lighter rocks. "What are You trying to tell me, God?" I cry out in frustration.

I am indeed more frustrated, but I feel this is one of those teachable moments on my hike up Monument Mountain. I search my mind for answers throughout the day and regret ever having stumbled upon that pile of rocks. I plop down discouraged and disgruntled. *Replacement rocks? What am I replacing?*

Several hours pass, and I come to the realization that pitching my rock on the ground was not enough. In my heart, I know what was weighing me down, but I don't know how to fix it other than throwing my rock into the pile. To lighten my load, I must replace my weighty rock with a smoother, lighter one. The only way to do that is to replace the word with something else. I grab my backpack, pull out the rock I had put back in, and look at the word I had scribbled—*fear.* Rushing over to the replacement rock pile, I pick up a smooth stone. On it I write two words—*confidence* and *trust.*

I place my new stone in my backpack and take my heavy rock over to the pile where other hikers have placed theirs. I put it on the pile. The rock is meant to stay there, not continue with me. My new stone will be with me until I reach the end. I hesitate because fear has been such a part of this hike thus far. Should I really leave it behind? Confidence and trust will have to replace fear. It's not easy leaving fear on the pile of rocks. Learning to have confidence in others and trusting God for healing is often a hard task maybe because of the setbacks I have experienced along the way. I go back to the pile of lighter stones and gather several more just in case I want to rid my backpack of any more weight.

Trust and confidence go hand in hand with replacing fear. Those two words on this stone will serve as a constant reminder to "Trust in the LORD with all your heart, and lean not unto your own understanding. In all your ways acknowledge him, and he will make straight your paths" (Proverbs 3:5–6 ESV). "The LORD will be your confidence and will keep your foot from being caught" (Proverbs 3:26 ESV).

Every now and again, I catch myself looking at the rock I threw down and wondering how this will affect my hike tomorrow. Will my load be lighter? The ultimate test will be whether I have the fortitude to leave my rock in the pile. I pray I don't go back to retrieve fear and make it a permanent part of my life.

Okay, God, I know I placed only one rock on the pile, but fear has been with me since the beginning, since I first heard the word *cancer*. I know I can't live my life in fear, so I ask You to help me leave fear behind and move forward with trust and confidence.

Morning comes all too quickly. It is the day I will hike to Trail Marker 23. I get up, put on my backpack, and head out. I didn't rest well last night. I kept thinking of what lay ahead. I wrestled with why God had given me this strenuous trail. If things had gone as planned, I would have been almost to the top of Monument Mountain by now, but setbacks reared their ugly heads, so I'm behind schedule. Well, my schedule—the one I think I should be on. But God always seems to have a different plan. I just can't figure things out. One second, things are on the upswing in life—for the first time in a very long time—and then the shocking news of a double mastectomy. My life comes to a screeching halt, and here I am hiking on unfamiliar trails.

It will take a few hours to make it to the next marker. The trail is not as rugged, but I don't feel like putting one foot in front of the other. I am so weary, so tired. I just want to quit. Of course, quitting is not an option. There's no turning back.

Hours pass, and I see the marker ahead, but I don't know if I can do this. I trudge forward with every ounce of energy I can muster and plop down in front of the sign reading Trail Marker 23.

Trail Marker 23
January 18, 2012

I saw Dr. Willard to get my stitches removed and expand the right tissue expander. I was looking forward to getting the stitches removed, but the other event—I'd heard it was painful. I spoke to Dr. Willard briefly, and Tammy set to work taking out my stitches. For some reason, I was more emotional that day than others. Probably lack of sleep. I was right about the tissue expander; it hurt. I was so ready to move on with my life! Judy held my hand while Tammy was working with the tissue expander. I was sold on the importance of the human touch during difficult times.

I realized I had not suffered as had those who had had to endure chemo or radiation. I thought that when the diagnosis was pre-cancer, the suffering was quieter. The loss was the same, but the suffering was not. I was emotionally raw. I had exposed my innermost self to people I really didn't know, which was not in my character. My tears flowed for no apparent reason. I found myself mulling over the last several months in the stillness of the night. I rummaged through the recesses of my mind for answers but found none.

Dr. Dasher saying "I have good news and bad" back in November replayed in my head. Every time I looked at my body, it was a stark reminder that I was not in control of my life or anything else for that matter.

God, I know You hear me, and that amazes me. Millions of people are asking You for something at the same time as I am, yet You hear us all. I am exhausted. I don't know how to ask for help or support. It's not that easy. The human touch, a voice of support, or the nearness of a friend is important during this season in my life. But everyone has a life of his or her own to live. Even my family has their own lives, and somehow, I don't feel a part of that world anymore because of this trial/trail. I know, God—I'm having a pity party for myself. Forgive me. I'm struggling with so many things today. All I can do is ask You to help me, to give me strength. I have nothing left.

Whew! What a hike! I am exhausted mentally, physically, and emotionally. I decide to stay here for a week or so. If I don't pull myself together, I won't be able to continue. As always, I see nooks and crannies where I can rest, reflect, and pray. When daylight dawns, I plan to mill around Trail Marker 23 and find what awaits me here. Until then, I will make a little fire, eat, and call it a day. I scrounge in my backpack and pull out my confidence and trust stone. I put it in my pocket as a reminder that fear can no longer be the word that dominates my hike.

The day has dawned. The sky is ominous; a storm may be brewing. Up to this point, I haven't had any bad weather; but weather can change quickly on a mountain such as this. I think the weather will keep me still for today, which is fine. I want extra time to read my journal, to see where I have been, and to organize my scattered thoughts of discouragement, fear, and despair. Today, I will reorganize and reflect. I have no way of knowing if the storm will happen, but I am prepared, sheltered in these rocks. The fire is still crackling, and I have food.

The wind is blowing, and the rain is falling. What a beautiful sound the raindrops make as they strum a leaf and fall to another in a melody all their own. It is a calming sound, but a storm is still in the making. I lean back on my backpack. My journal in hand, I begin to go through it page by page from Trail Marker 1 to Trail Marker 23. I read carefully reflecting on every word as if it happened today. Devastating words, discouraging words, judgmental words, gentle words, compassionate words, and healing words all have played their roles during my hike. As I rest, I challenge myself to find what has changed in my life. I started strong, but my pace has slowed down considerably, and I don't feel as brave or as strong as I did back then.

I am keenly aware that things changed at Trail Markers 16 and 17. The words I heard felt like a bomb dropped on my soul: "It's only a setback, not a disaster." No one understood the ramifications of what was said that day except me. I reread the journal entry from Trail Markers 16 and 17 again and again. As the rain starts to fall harder, things start coming together in my mind. I read those journal entries and those that follow countless times. I had become a failure. The setback has truly become a disaster in my life. I have failed my family, friends, doctor, nurses, and God by not being able to overcome this setback. No matter how hard I tried, I don't overcome this obstacle. I have failed miserably, and my failure is paralyzing me from the inside out.

The wind is picking up. It won't be long before the storm is upon me.

Thunder vibrates the core of my being. It's like feeling fireworks on the Fourth of July. I go back to my journal. My desire is to finish this strenuous hike, so where does the real problem lie? My eyes are heavy as is my heart as I push myself farther up into the shelter. God's rain song provides a lullaby that allows me get some much-needed rest.

I awake feeling refreshed. My mind is clearer. The rain is still falling at a pretty good clip. Thunder rumbles throughout the mountain. What was I trying to figure out before I nodded off? Oh yeah. What transpired between Trail Marker 16 to the place where I am now has me in despair. Thunder rolls throughout the mountain once again like an orchestral piece written just for me. The sky is dark, so I know the storm is fast approaching.

Storms—I love 'em! The thunder. The lightning. The rain. Storms can be life-threatening. They can produce winds that can destroy neighborhoods. Lightning can kill, and rain can cause flooding. I feel a storm brewing in me. This storm is powerful. It started brewing back on Trail Markers 16 and 17 when I heard the word *setback*. I didn't realize a storm was on its way. I wasn't prepared. I hadn't factored in setbacks of any kind; thus, the reason the storm in my life is out of control.

I have had many stormy days in my life, even in these past months, but no storm has ever touched my life with such force as the one I am in now. Trail Marker 17 was only the threat of the storm, but I believed in my heart it would blow over. Since I saw it only as a threat, I did nothing to prepare myself should it intensify. When the threat became reality, I felt threatened and alone. I was drowning in fear and sorrow. The thunderous word *setback* shook my soul, and the lightning was striking fear and doubt in my heart.

As I reread these journal entries, I understand the storm in my life has the potential to become dangerous, even deadly. As long as this personal storm intensifies, I cannot apply the principles I am learning to my life. I find myself on Trail Marker 23 realizing the storm in my soul has gotten worse. I never expected a storm. Whatever possessed me to think I would trudge right up Monument Mountain without any difficulties? My word! It's a strenuous hike. Even seasoned hikers have difficulties on strenuous trails. With real storms, people have the sense to seek shelter and observe the storm from a safe location. It's no different with personal life storms. The safest location in a personal storm is in God's Word.

In Matthew 8:23–27 and Mark 4:35–41, the disciples were with Jesus when the storm blew up. The waves were tossing the boat to and fro, and Jesus was doing what? Sleeping. His disciples were in a panic. The storm frightened them; they thought they would die even with Jesus there. We might fault those guys for their fear, but what about you and me? They woke Jesus up and said, "Teacher, do you not care that we are perishing?" (ESV). No more than you do, I don't want to admit that I have asked Jesus a similar question about my trail/trail. We all have asked Jesus this question in some way or another— "Don't you care that …" In the midst of our unbelief comes His gentle voice, "Peace! Be Still! And the wind ceased, and there was a great calm" (ESV).

From looking back at all my journal entries, I see that the one thing that has remained constant is His care for me. The storm came when I began to dwell on the word *setback*. So many times, I have asked the same question the disciples did: "Teacher, do you not care that I am perishing, alone, scared, discouraged, and filled with fear?" A host of times, He has spoken through a friend, a doctor, and a superb doctor's staff the very words He said to the storm—"Peace! Be still!" He alone calms the storms in our souls, but He uses people to help diffuse the fear, loneliness, and discouragement by coming alongside us with words of encouragement, a gentle touch, a text or phone call, a cup of coffee, a quick lunch, or the commitment to continue hiking alongside me. All these acts of kindness are reminders of how if we are available, He can use the simplest things to speak peace and calmness over a storm-tossed soul.

The rain stops. Sunshine filters through the trees illuminating the mountain and bringing it to life after the storm. Isn't that how God does His children? We can be in a storm, call out to Him, and expect a great calm to illuminate our hearts and minds. Does this mean there will not be any more storms? No, but this is one of those teachable moments when Jesus looks at me just as He did the disciples and asks, "Have you still no faith?"

From Trail Marker 1 to now, He has been faithful. I pull out one of the smooth stones I took from the previous trail marker and write the word *faithfulness*. I place the stone in my pocket and thank God for His faithfulness to me during this storm in my life. His voice resonates in my heart—"Peace! Be still!"

It is time to move forward. I have sat in this spot for over a week. I have faced myself head-on in a battle, in a raging storm brewing in my soul. I have struggled at times to hear "Peace! Be still!" I have found myself looking into my soul trying to reach deep down to survive the rest of this hike. Each day of reflecting has come with a new challenge—facing who I really am in light of this trial. This has been a difficult week.

On January 24, 2012, I finally get up enough nerve to call a place called Second to Nature. It's a store where women who have had mastectomies can purchase wigs, hats, clothing, and prosthetics. I went there because Dr. Willard has started expanding my right side, and I feel so lopsided. I feel like the Scarecrow in the Wizard of Oz when his straw fell out. I was looking for some way to feel whole. I walk in, fill out all the necessary papers for insurance, and then am escorted to a fitting room. Once again, I lay myself bare in front of someone I don't know.

I think the hardest part for me was going to this place. I went alone. There are some things that are personal, and I knew this would be one of those moments. After I purchased what I needed, I sat in the car and wept. This whole event—from having the surgery, to the emotional roller-coaster, to shopping in this store—devastates me. I am crying so hard that I get lost going home. I couldn't even hear the GPS giving me directions.

What I am learning from this event is how hard people—not just me—fight to look normal or to have some normalcy in their lives. Most everyone in that store had had the same surgery as I had; some were going through chemo while others were fighting for their lives, but we were all looking for the same thing—wholeness.

Today, January 26, 2012, has been a horrible day. I wonder why God doesn't allow me to die. What good am I to anyone? What purpose does any of this serve? I believe the word *compassion* is a foreign word for so many. Those often closest to the situation cannot hear the silent tears dripping as I type these words, nor can they see the pain tearing at my soul. Everyone is doing his or her own thing. In many cases, suffering is silent because we turn a deaf ear to it. Many suffer silently—children who are abused, women who find themselves raising a family single-handedly, men who have lost their spouses, the terminally ill, and those who grieve over the loss of someone or something. This is not an extensive list, but it gives you and me an idea of how often we have turned a deaf ear to those in need.

Just when the storm in my soul seems to calm down, another one comes on stronger and harder. I haven't been able to escape the storm today. It's bearing down stronger and stronger. Though I am screaming, "Master, don't you care that I am drowning?" the waves of sorrow and pain hit harder against my heart. I don't feel very courageous about making the trek to Trail Marker 24. I just want to quit. I'm weary of making decisions alone. I'm tired of insensitive people trying to convince me that my sickness is strictly due to sin. I'm up with not being able to fix the problem with my body. I'm overcome with loneliness. I'm worn out. I have tried to be upbeat and positive, but the hike has been cruel in so many ways.

I look at my two stones, *faithfulness* written on one and *trust* and *confidence* on the other. I shove them into my backpack. Today, my soul is a miserable mess, I sit alone—par for the course almost every day. If I don't start moving toward the next trail marker, I'll be inclined to quit. Silent tears blur my vision as I put the last things in my pack. I hate all of this—the loneliness, the pain, the lack of compassion by some, accusations, and the upcoming surgeries. What is there to love about this hike? I'm screaming for help, but no one hears me.

God, today is miserable! My heart aches because I am so lonely. I have no one to talk to. I am alone looking at four walls as is the case every day. I just want this to be over, but for some reason, I can't get over that infection, and setbacks have occurred. I don't know why You didn't heal that crazy infection. I know You could have, but You didn't. My family is hurting, and nothing seems to be changing for the better. Financially, we're are at our limit. I can't work. What good am I to anyone? Everyone has his or her own life to live.

What purpose does this serve? I have asked why a thousand times, but no answer is given. I have prayed earnestly, faithfully, and with great intensity for good to come from this, but something's wrong. The storm raging in my soul is more than I can deal with. The tears come more frequently along with the heartbreak of being so excluded from the daily things of life. My fight is about gone. Unless You rescue me today, I don't know what will happen.

January 26, 2012

I'm on my way to pick up Jonathan from school. Yes, I'm still crying. While driving, I'm praying, almost yelling, asking God again, "What purpose does all this serve? Why doesn't anyone care? Couldn't You let just one person care?"

And then it happens—my phone alerts me to a text. Rosa is inviting me and my family to her house for coffee and dinner. Coincidence? I don't think so. I got to the end of my rope today. My thoughts are working against me. I don't know how or why God did this for me, but it was a wonderful night of fellowship.

Trail Marker 24 is just ahead. I see it in the distance. The hike has been difficult as I have fallen over roots and slipped on rocks and leaves. It took me a long time to move from where I was to get within eyeshot of Trail Marker 24. Yesterday sure had its share of problems, tears, and setbacks, but today is a new day. I press on.

Trail Marker 24

January 27, 2012

I saw Dr. Willard hopefully to get a tentative date for surgery and to expand my right side. I was hoping it would be the last time. I had my list of questions. A tentative surgery date was scheduled for February 27. Becky was desperately trying to get the insurance to agree to allow me to have the surgery in the office. We would wait for the answer. Expansion is over for the right side—Yeah! I wished all of this would end soon.

I will stay here for several weeks. I have noticed with each trail marker, my stay gets a little longer. Maybe God is trying to slow me down so I can hear His voice. It is very nice up here. The view is stunning. The past several weeks have exhausted me beyond description. The storm raging in me has hurt my progress. I have to change my attitude if I want to continue my journey. I have allowed my adventure to become an annoyance, so anger and impatience have challenged me to quit. When anger and impatience come to the forefront of any area of our lives, they cause us to react in ways that don't please God.

Survival. I'm learning this is what it takes to make it up Monument

Mountain. It takes more than knowing how to navigate a trail, find food, keep warm, and understand weather conditions. It takes mental, physical, and emotional stamina. It's all about attitude. My attitude will either make me or break me. To survive, I must adjust my thinking, my attitude, to fit the situation. When I started on this hike, my attitude and focus were different. I had more energy, and I hadn't experienced any significant setbacks. My attitude and focus changed when the situation around me changed. When I heard the word *setback*, I wanted to quit. Even die.

When I realized I couldn't control my situation, my thinking process changed. I no longer wanted to move forward. My attitude blinded me to the fact that trust, confidence, and faithfulness were all still a part of this journey up Monument Mountain. Surviving this trail has not been without obstacle—silent tears, loneliness, setbacks, fear, discouragement, and pain. On many days, these obstacles kept me from making progress or hindered me from learning lessons. What obstacles or blockades are you allowing into your life that might hinder you from moving in the direction God wants you to move?

The sun rises over Monument Mountain. I will use today to find a way around these obstacles that I pray will help me survive the rest of this hike. I have been doing a lot of thinking about obstacles. As I think about the word *obstacle*, I visualize it as an obstacle course. I think how different an obstacle course for a child is from that of a Marine during basic training. Again, the concept of starting out with something easy and moving to something strenuous is seen not only in the area of hiking but also in handling obstacles. Obstacles are a test of our ability to endure what lies ahead of us.

I am also trying to figure out if there is a difference between the extra baggage I carry and the obstacles I face. The more I think on the matter, the more I'm inclined to believe that obstacles are often put in my way to provide new strength whereas the baggage I carry is a choice. I decide to allow myself to be hindered by my backpack. Once I conquer an obstacle, I gain confidence and a fresh sense of hope. There is so much to think and pray about before moving on to the next trail marker.

I open my journal to a fresh page and write this.

> February 9, 2012: Today is Wednesday. I have been thinking a lot about obstacles and their purpose during this strenuous hike. Last night, after all that was left of the fire was the glow of embers and I was still and silent, I had time to think. The obstacles I have encountered are like stones—hard, unforgiving. They are in my way—hard to maneuver around—yet useful when I need to step on something to give me stability when climbing a steep hill. The stones gave me the ability to move higher.
>
> I have wanted to quit, to just give up. I have not understood why God doesn't make things easier instead of more strenuous. I wondered why God didn't remove the stones from the path and just make them straight and easy. I have given much thought to this especially after the storm I just endured. God provides balance in my life. Currently, I am blessed to have things calm following the storm. Tears are often followed by laughter, and rain is followed by sunshine. The calm, laughter, and sunshine level the path for a while. They're God's way of giving me balance in turbulent times.

While I was lying there, I realized something very important. My strenuous hike hasn't always been filled with rocky places. Many times, I've hiked on level paths. The more I thought about that, the more God revealed to me that it is through the encouragement of friends—their texts, emails, face-to-face conversations, phone calls—who have made the path level. They are the ones who bring calmness, laughter, and sunshine. God uses people to bring balance when things seem unsteady.

I received an email from my friend today. It was titled "Don't Waste Your Pain." Only God knew what had been revealed to me in the stillness of the night, but the email confirmed what I was learning—balance during difficult and strenuous hikes comes from God blessing us with wonderful friends who are not afraid to reach out or hike alongside us.

Psalm 91:11–12 (NASB) reads, "For He will give His angels charge concerning you, to guard you in all your ways. They will bear you up in their hands, that you do not strike your foot against a stone." God doesn't promise to remove the stones in our paths, but He promises to make them stepping stones, not stumbling blocks. I can use the stones to move higher because of the difficulties I face.

What I have learned thus far on the trail is that storms and stones serve a purpose. There's a calm after the storm called friendship and family. The stones are not obstacles but stepping stones that allow me to continue my climb up Monument Mountain. These past few days have been an eye-opener regarding the person I really am. I'm not strong. In fact, I'm a needy human being.

Night falls on Monument Mountain. I need a place to rest. I go back to the spot I encountered when I first arrived here and lay my backpack down. It is time to rest and reflect. It won't be long before I'll move from this trail marker to the next. Each one is just a little harder to hike due to the intensity of the path, so it will be hard to leave here after so much time to rest and think.

Today, I will press on toward Trail Marker 25. It has been several weeks since I have felt the weight of my backpack. Trail Marker 24 came with many hardships. I have felt things in my heart I have never felt. Thoughts I never thought I was capable of thinking have crossed my mind. It's time to move out and leave this place realizing stones and storms serve their purposes in times of trials.

Trail Marker 25
Wednesday, February 15, 2012

I had a pre-op appointment with Dr. Willard. I had a list of questions. Tammy took my blood pressure and weighed me. She went over a packet of material pertaining to the surgery. She handed me five prescriptions to be filled before surgery. Dr. Willard listened to my heart and lungs. I took out my questions. "How long will I be out of commission?" I don't even know why I asked that. When I heard "Four weeks," I about croaked.

"Okay, next question. Explain the surgical procedure to me. How will you cut me? Where will the drain tube be?"

He drew a picture for me. "The cut will not be as big. I'm farther over to the side. The drain will go in the same place as last time. It'll go in the same spot."

I'd saved the big question for last. "Be honest. How hard will it be to make me look normal? To make both sides even?"

Dr. Willard looked me in the eyes and said with compassion, "It won't be too hard." He told me how careful I would have to be. "Don't be a couch potato, but don't be up doing too much. I want you to heal. I do this surgery all the time, but you're a special case. I won't say everything will be okay this time. We're just going to wait it out."

I was more afraid of going to surgery that time than I had been in December; maybe it was because I knew what was ahead of me. "Make sure you let people help you," he said. Oh yeah, not easy instructions for a girl like me. I'd had several weeks of the sheer bliss of cooking, playing, visiting friends, and he wanted me to go into reverse for a few weeks.

I left the doctor's office not feeling very confident. The last place I wanted this surgery was in the hospital, but insurance wouldn't agree. I was scared. Simple as that. I wanted this surgery to be successful. I had asked God so many times why, but He hadn't revealed an answer. I was not sure if the words I heard that day carried life or death, but they were hard words to hear, hard words to heed.

Trekking to this trail marker was quite difficult. I kept slipping and falling. At one point, I slide so far down that I don't think I'll be able to climb back up. My hands are bloody from trying to break my fall. I am bruised and battered. I am so ready to reach the top. Some days, I don't think it is even within reach, but I must try. I'm sore and exhausted. I'm tired of fighting a battle I didn't volunteer to be in. I'm not a very good soldier. I want to retreat, but obviously, that's not an option.

I have twelve days to be here before I approach Trail Marker 26, which according to the map will be a hard climb and a difficult place to stay. I will study my map and look for clues that will help me as the countdown to Trail Marker 26 begins. Looking at the map, I learn I need to move out from where I am hunkered down quicker than anticipated. According to the map, when I have seven days left, I am to head to Trail Marker 26. There are seven stops, one for each day so I can rest. Each day will serve a specific purpose. Today is the beginning of the seventh day, so I guess I better head out.

Day 7: February 21, 2012

I have my backpack ready and map in hand. I am to hike until I come to a place marked with a *C*. I'll rest there and get ready to move out the next day. The trail is steep, and I'm exhausted mentally and physically. I wonder why the trail is laid out this way. It would make better sense if the trek to Trail Marker 26 was in one fell swoop as opposed to stopping and starting, but I'll follow the instructions. I have hiked all day. Emotionally, my mind is becoming weaker knowing that in seven days, the trail will become excruciatingly painful. I finally approach the place marked with a *C* and take in my new surroundings.

This place seems okay. The *C* is hanging on a stick with a small sign above it telling me to remove the letter and take it to the next location. Done. None of this makes much sense, but I am so tired by the hike, by thinking, by the weariness of the day. I put the letter in my backpack and pull out my journal.

God, nothing makes sense to me right now. I am frightened about reaching Trail Marker 26. Hiking there comes with much dread and much fear. I have tried to talk to You about these things, but I feel so alone. The next seven days will be hard. I don't know if I can make it. I just want to be finished. Please God, have mercy on me and get me through the next seven days.

With that written, I call it a night and prepare for the next day's journey.

Day 6: February 22, 2012

Barely slept last night due to the anticipation of reaching the next place. The map indicates the place will be marked with an *O* this time. I gather my things. Once again, I'm on my way up the slippery trail exhausted, so progress will be slow. I am reminded of the children's story of the tortoise and the hare. I feel like the tortoise today—slow and steady. I press forward. After many hours, I see the *O* hanging on a stick marking the place where I will rest. The instructions are the same, so I put the letter in my backpack.

I don't know where to begin as the days tick down. The silence in this spot is eerie. It's like being in a room with a clock ticking—a subtle reminder that six days is all I have left before I look fear in the face again.

God, I've made it this far. You have always provided for me during these times. You have provided friends with words of life along Eagle Height Trail from the beginning. I don't understand why this time is so difficult. I'm inching my way closer to the top, but I don't feel I'm making progress. What's wrong with me? Between You and me, God, You know what things are like in my life—great fear and sadness felt from everyone. How many times I've wanted them to hike alongside me, but it hasn't happened because this isn't their mountain to climb. Maybe that's why I'm so lonely. I'm trying to keep my head up in the midst of this difficult time, but I'm running out of steam. The silence reiterates how alone I feel. God, all I can do now is to beg You to help me.

Silent tears fall to the ground. Tears no one will ever see or hear.

Day 5: February 23, 2012

The morning suns shines through the trees and awakens me to a new day. Each day, it gets harder to pack my things and move toward the next trail marker. I pull out my map. I am looking for a place marked with a *U* this time. I find it very odd how things are marked on this trail. I fold my map and head up hoping the hike will not take hours.

My mind is in overdrive. Five days is all that is left before I reach an uncertain destination. I am constantly telling myself things will be okay, but I find it harder and harder to believe my self-pep talks. One of the many things God is teaching me as I hike this strenuous trail is the importance of encouraging others. Here again, our words hold the power of life and death. I have had plenty of time on this journey to hear, read, and speak words. Some have hurt me deeply, but many have been life giving, spoken at a time when I felt I couldn't take another step up this mountain.

I find the place I am to stop for the night. I have found the letter *U* and place it with the others in my backpack. I listen to the crackling of the fire. I pull out my map and see where I am to stop tomorrow. I will be looking for a place marked with an *R*. The fire provides the physical but not the emotional warmth I desperately need as Trail Marker 26 approaches. I pull out my Bible to find comfort and help. Encouraging others has been on my mind as I have hiked for many hours today, a lesson I personally need to heed.

In 1 Thessalonians 5:11 (NASB), I read, "Therefore, encourage one another and build up one another, just as you also are doing." When I reach the top of Monument Mountain, my life will be forever changed, but getting there hasn't been easy.

God, today, I need encouragement. I have found Your Word to be of help and comfort. I know You have a specific plan for me—I am struggling with the upcoming event on February 28. Please provide for me today. It gets mighty lonely here. Days are long and wearisome. Everything I do I do alone. Please send someone along today. I do love You, Lord, with all my heart. I feel overwhelmed, but You know my thoughts.

Day 4: February 24, 2012

Up extremely early. Just couldn't sleep. Too much going through my head about reaching Trail Marker 26. I pull out my map to see where need to go today. I am looking for an *R* today. I pull out the letters I have collected thus far—C, O, U. I pull out my journal before I leave and write these letters down. I don't know what they mean, so I decide to make up something for each letter, something to carry me through. C—chin up, don't quit. O—organize your thoughts. U—understand this is part of God's plan. I throw my things in my backpack and head out.

The trail is narrow. I wish I had someone to talk to, but things don't always work the way I want them to. This hike has been strenuous and extremely lonely, but I am learning to rely on God for so many things. The desire of my heart is to reach the top of Monument Mountain a better person than when I started the trek. Each step on this narrow path is tough; I have to be aware of each or risk slipping and falling. The way is not easy, but my prayer today has been, "Please, God, provide." That's all I know to ask at this point.

The *R* is ahead. I have hiked nearly half the day. I am drained physically and mentally. I am glad I reached this spot before darkness fell. I grab the *R* and place it in my backpack. R—rely on His strength, not your own.

I can see all around the mountain. I can see clearly parts of the winding trail I have been following these past four months. Only four months have gone by, yet it seems longer. But it seems like yesterday I heard the words, "I have good news and bad news." Strange how my mind remembers the freshness of those words. They still bring tears to my eyes and pain to my heart, the worst nightmare ever.

I'll rest my eyes after I get a small fire started and a snack to eat. It has been four long, hard days. Hiking many miles back to back with just a little rest in between is hard on the body. Once I have rested, I will look to see what tomorrow holds on my map.

Day 3: February 25, 2012

Today is packed with nothing but hiking. I got a really late start, and all I know is I am headed for a place marked with an *A*. I hate being in a panic. I have many hours in front of me. The path is even narrower than before, and it's all I can do to carry the load on my back.

God, if ever I needed You to help me with this trail, it is now. I cannot do this alone. It's all I can do to move under my load. Please get me to this place of rest safely. I am so tired.

I finally arrive. The letter is hanging on a stick as were the others. I grab it. After putting my backpack down, I get a small fire going. It's mighty cool, and there's a breeze. I hope there's not a storm brewing. I get out my journal and again read through the whole thing. I am amazed at the miles I have traveled; where I started seemed tough, but that was nothing in comparison to now. I have written down something for each of the letters I've picked up, so A—act, don't react. I need to act on God's principles and His promises, not react to things around me, but that's easier said than done.

I must sleep. Sleep has not come easy these past few days. I pull out my map to measure how far I will have to travel tomorrow. Looks like a whole day of walking up steep terrain. I don't think I can do this. Tomorrow, I'll be looking for the letter *G* to mark my resting spot.

Day 2: February 26, 2012

No sleep came to my eyes no matter how hard I tried. Each day, my body becomes wearier. I feel my life is being sucked from me. I dump everything out of my backpack so I can reorganize it. Let's see. I have carried my Bible, journal, basic hiking stuff, and rocks the past four months. I put the rocks on which I wrote "trust and confidence" and "faithfulness" in my pocket. I'll need them to move on. Okay, I'm ready. My backpack isn't lighter, but it's neater.

Night is upon me. I can barely see the trail. I have followed the map correctly, but I seem to be lost. Panic is not in a hiker's vocabulary. I have to take a minute and assess my situation. I shine my little flashlight on the map. I'm not lost. The place I'm looking for appears to be up ahead. I shine the light on the trail and keep moving. Darkness has come along with all the night sounds I once found scary but now find comfort in. I shine the light around and up ahead I see the letter I have been waiting for. I take the *G* from the stick, pull out my journal, and write "G—give God glory in all things good and bad."

Darkness covers the sky like a thick blanket. I crawl next to the fire and rest my head on my backpack. Too weary to look at the map. I shut my eyes and beg God for rest. I know tomorrow will be extra hard since it leaves me only one day before reaching Trail Marker 26.

Day 1: February 27, 2012

It is early. The sun hasn't begun to peek over the mountain. Another restless night. It's not good going into the last leg of the hike without sleep. My mind is active making lists of things I feel have to be accomplished before reaching Trail Marker 26. I pull out my map and try to see what I should look for today and how long I'll be on the trail.

Unfortunately, the map doesn't give me a clear sign of where I'll need to stop. All the other times, I was given a letter to alert me, but now, nothing. It seems the trail is winding and extremely narrow, so I better get started. I hope there will be a sign of some sort to alert me to the exact spot I will need to stop. With my two rocks in my pocket, I sling my backpack on my back and trudge forward. My emotions are high, and my tears stain the ground. What's strange is that I know I have to do this, but it's so difficult.

Hours pass. My progress is slow. Tears blurring my vision make it harder to travel the path set before me. I can't do it. I just can't do it. The pain, the loneliness, the tears—they're becoming more than I can bear. The silence is deafening. I just can't do it.

God, I can't do it. I'm scared. O God, I am so lonely. What I face tomorrow is too hard. Why, God, does it have to be the way it has been? I want all this to go away. I'm scared, God. Please help me.

I come to a small spot that appears to be where I will stop. There is still daylight, so I can look around for clues. Since all the other spots had letters to indicate a stopping point, I figure something has to be around here to show me I'm in the right place. I take off my backpack, get a little fire started, and start accessing my spot. Tucked inside some rocks is a piece of paper that I read.

> Today, you have reached your last destination before moving on to Trail Marker 26 tomorrow. You have done well and have proven you can accomplish more than you think. Along the way, your map gave instructions to look for letters to mark the places where you would find rest before the next day's journey. You have found the correct place today. Put the letters on the ground in the order you got them. Your last letter is concealed in an envelope under a rock where you entered.

I take out all my letters and arrange them as instructed—C, O, U, R, A, and G. I go back to the place where I entered and look for the rock where an envelope is hidden. I look under several rocks before finding the envelope. I slowly I open it. Inside is the letter *E* with a note attached to it.

> Dear friend, place this letter at the end of the others you have collected along the way. This word spells out what God promises to give you for tomorrow's journey. In fact, He has given this to you every time you have moved to hike to a different place. Look up Joshua 1:9 and find what you need to get through the difficult hike tomorrow.

The letters spell the word *courage*. I pull out my Bible and read Joshua 1:9 (ESV): "Have I not commanded you? 'Be strong and courageous. Do not be frightened, and do not be dismayed, for the LORD your God is with you wherever you go.'" The words *wherever you go* mean more to me right now than anyone will ever know. Today, I will cling to those three words, for tomorrow, I will need courage. I take out a smooth rock from my backpack and write "courage," on it, and put in it my pocket to remind me He will give me courage for my journey tomorrow. I pull out my journal and write, "E—expect God to do above what you ask or think."

God, I still don't understand all of this. You alone will have to provide the courage I will need for tomorrow. I'm empty, alone, and scared.

Trail Marker 26

February 28, 2012

I was facing surgery number four. I was fearful, but I'd had many days to think about where this journey has taken me. I asked God for one thing before I went to the operating room—to see at least one familiar face before I was put under. God provided in an extraordinary way. I saw Staci, the nurse anesthetist; Becky, the surgical nurse; and Dr. Willard. I found great comfort in seeing and talking to them.

Surgery went well, and I went home around noon. I was anticipating that God would do great things and that no infection would rear its ugly head. I followed Dr. Willard's orders, and I would see him on Friday, March 2 to remove the drain tube.

Getting to this point on the trail has been more difficult than ever. My mind has fought through jungles of deceitful tales breathed from the mouth of the devil. He asked me multiple times, "Did God really say He would help you?" There have been times when I couldn't see a way out and my mind thought things contrary to what I knew was biblically true. The machete of truth is harder to use in times of adversity than I expected. Discouragement, depression, fear, and self-pity are all jungle-like vines that entangle the mind, The machete of truth—God's Word—has to be applied or defeat will be the ultimate winner.

I found it extremely challenging to encourage myself during these past days. I think God is teaching me many things, one of which is to rely on Him and the promise that He will provide exactly what I need. I am learning a lot about the person I used to be and the person I am becoming. Hard times have the opportunity if I allow them to make me a stronger person. Some days are better than others. Silent tears speak for the loneliness I have felt today. The stillness is almost too much to handle.

I am glad that each resting spot was marked by a letter and that the word *courage* wasn't spelled out at the beginning. I don't think I would have believed Joshua 1:9 before I reached that trail marker. I am waiting to hear from God again and find out what He has in store for me. I'm waiting to stand back and gaze on His glory and what He has planned for me through this strenuous hike. I will rest here and move out soon to Trail Marker 27.

Trail Marker 27
March 2, 2012

I had an appointment with Dr. Willard to remove the drain tube. Things seemed to be going fine. The tube came out, and no infection was evident. We talked about so many things. I was thankful for a doctor who listened to me and genuinely cared about me. The marching orders I've been given the past four months have not been easy, but I'm thankful God provided encouraging words through nurses, doctors, and friends when I needed them.

Getting to Trail Marker 27 wasn't too strenuous. I hiked it without any problems. The path was quite level. I'll stay here for another day and then go to the next trail marker. I'm somewhat anxious about that one; the trail is kind of rocky. It's time to rest. God has given me courage thus far, and I'm clinging to that as I lay my head down for the night.

I cannot explain the place where I am right now in my life. I cannot call it a place of contentment, yet I feel at peace. As I lie here covered by the darkness, I know God has a plan for me. What it is I do not know, but I'm willing to do whatever He is calling me to do.

Trail Marker 28
March 6, 2012

I spotted some redness around the left breast area and was overcome with fear—fear that infection might be returning. Fear of losing another tissue expander. Fear of Dr. Willard not being able to help me. Fear comes with the package of the unknown. I made an appointment to make sure there was no cause for alarm. And believe me, my fear alarm was ringing. Dr. Willard understood how paranoid I was especially after all I had experienced with infection.

He wasn't upset that I had come by and assured me I was okay. I had a hidden agenda. Rosa was leaving March 20, and if Dr. Willard gave me a good report, there was the possibility I could go with her. I had never flown, and I needed a break from being under house arrest. I was asking God for a miracle.

March 6, 2012 would probably be one of the most significant milestones in my life. I still had a long way to go in the process of healing, but Dr. Willard okayed my going with Rosa. Rosa's face was filled with happiness and hope. She booked the flight. In thirteen days, I'd make my first flight with my friend. I was so excited I could barely stand it. I would continue to pray for zero infection and that my body did not reject the tissue expander.

What a hike this has been. I have made it to two significant trail markers in a short time. God has been very gracious to me by giving me courage and now hope. I plunder through my backpack, pull out another rock, and write the word *hope* on it. I now have five words that symbolize my journey thus far: *trust*, *confidence*, *faithfulness*, *courage*, and *hope*. I take out another rock and write two words that should have been written from the start: *friendship* and *family*. God always knows the importance of friendship and family.

March 20, 2012

I didn't sleep a wink last night; I was too excited. Rosa will be here shortly to pick me up to go to the airport. I am nervous but also excited. I am not sure what to expect; but Rosa will give me clear instructions. It will be so nice to get away from the rut I have been in for several months.

My heart was pounding as we headed through the gate and off to the plane. The flight was nothing like I had expected, so I wonder why I was so fearful. Fear of the unknown is what I have experienced almost daily since my hike began. The view is unbelievable now that the sun is rising. I am amazed at the handiwork of God.

Due to fog, we were rerouted to Hartford, Connecticut, where we waited for the fog to lift in New York. We reached Baltimore around 1:30 p.m. We're staying near the Inner Harbor within walking distance of everything. Rosa will do her conference thing, and I will tour the unknown. What an adventure I am on!

We had such a great time. We found this little restaurant called Noodles and Co. The food was excellent. We ate lunch there twice, ate at a Spanish restaurant—crab soup, crab cakes, dessert, coffee. We visited the aquarium and Barnes & Noble, and we enjoyed friendship. I don't think I could ask God for anything better right now. I am feeling better and getting stronger each day, and this trip has been such a blessing. Rosa will never know how much this trip means to me. I learned a lot about people and myself—people I met and saw from day to day.

While Rosa was at her conference, I sat on a bench near the harbor and talked to people. Each person I encountered came from a different walk of life—some without jobs, some who hated their jobs, and many who were homeless. It was quite the experience, and not one time was I bored.

The trip home was unique. We left earlier than expected, and our seats on our first flight were not together. I had a nice time talking with the guy next to me. We landed in Charlotte, where we experienced another delay. I didn't mind. I enjoy having time to think and talk. I'll be glad to get home, back to life, picking up at home right where I left off.

Trail Marker 29
March 29, 2012

I had an appointment with Dr. Willard to start filling up the left tissue expander. It wasn't extremely painful. My prayer is to continue to move forward and make great progress.

Time passes slowly as I hike. Each day, I am faced with new challenges as I progress up Monument Mountain. I have no time to rest. In a week,

I am to be at the next trail marker. The path is still narrow; maneuvering around roots, rocks, and fallen trees continues to be a challenge. Tonight, I will plan how far I will hike each day based on the nature of the trail. I am not as strong as I was when I started this journey.

Fortunately, I find a good place to stop for the evening. I am comforted by the sounds of tree frogs calling out in the night and the light of my fire. It is peaceful here.

God, I want to be able to say, "Wherever He leads, I'll go" and mean it. I struggle everyday with loneliness. I wonder if I'll make it to the top of Monument Mountain. I wonder what lies ahead. What will become of this whole hiking adventure? God, I need You.

The wind is blowing gently through the trees and playing a goodnight song. I am so tired. My body screams at me to rest. It won't be long until I reach Trail Marker 30. I'm not sure how I feel about many things, but I hope a good night's rest will give me a better idea of what actions I need to take.

Morning comes all too quickly. I sit still and reflect on the journey. It hasn't been easy. I pull out my rocks and arrange them. Five rocks, seven words, each rock significant to my journey. I pick up each one and remember where I was on this hike when I wrote the words on each rock. Sometimes, I was struggling, but God had provided. Other times, He was quiet and I had to search for meaning. But in the end, I grew. I cling to the rock with the word *hope* and remember when I finally felt hope. That changed my perspective and attitude about whether I could continue. Hope is the light God gives when discouragement snuffs out the flicker of light in the heart.

I put the smooth stone with the word *hope* in my pocket. I gather my things and head for the trail. Just another's day journey before I reach Trail Marker 30. It takes great effort to resume hiking on this narrow path.

I hike for quite some time before I catch my breath as the incline steepens. I sip fresh water to quench my parched lips. I reach in my pocket and feel the stone. Hope. I remember March 6, 2012 as if it were yesterday, the day hope revived itself in my heart. Pulling off the trail is refreshing, and I remember that God moves and works through the lives of others. "Iron sharpens iron" as it says in Proverbs 27:17 (NASB).

Nightfall. I need to stop. The trail, although demanding, has brought me to a place to rest. I see Trail Marker 30 just ahead. I get a small fire going and prepare a bite to eat. I pull out my journal. I read my entry from October 29, 2011. What a day that was; I was given the assignment of hiking this strenuous trail. I continue to read up to Trail Marker 29.

Father, I thank You for loving me. You have provided unseen hands to lift me up when I was not able to stand. You provided the light of friendship when days were dark. Your Word gave me comfort in the night when tears stung my cheeks. How great You are! Continue to guide me as the way is so narrow, amen.

Trail Marker 30
April 4, 2012

I had an appointment with Dr. Willard. He expanded the left tissue expander. It was a hard appointment. The pain was excruciating. Tears streamed down my face as I tried to recuperate. The pain was so bad that I called my parents to meet me at a restaurant just until I could pull myself together.

My parents had accompanied me every step of my way. They gave completely of themselves by coming and supporting me at a moment's notice. I didn't know why the day had been so emotional. I sat in my car and cried out to God, "Why?" He knew my frailties but still loved me. I could not wrap my mind around the past six months—they were like a bad dream. But God was not finished with me yet. He had a plan for me. As hard as this had been, I just wanted to do what He required of me.

Hope is what I am clinging to as I leave Trail Marker 30. I just don't know if I can continue. Trail Marker 31 isn't that far away, but I'm exhausted. I push forward on this narrow path. My mind is constantly thinking, reflecting, and wondering.

I wonder about Trail Marker 31. The sun is shining through the trees, birds are chirping, and new foliage is growing. I see hope in all these things. Each trail marker has presented its share of difficulties, but with

God's help, I have survived. I pull to the side of the trail to set up camp for the night. It is still daylight. I don't feel rushed; I'm enjoying everything around me.

There's a quaint waterfall nearby. It's beautiful and relaxing. I need some time to relax and catch up in my journal. After making sure I have enough firewood for the night and setting up my space, I head to the waterfall. What an alluring little spot tucked back from the trail not visible but audible. Listening to the waterfall relaxes every muscle. I take my socks and shoes off and stick my feet in the cool water.

I lean back on the damp rocks and hear God's silent sermon to my heart loudly. God is using nature to assure me He is the Creator. My mind is drawn to Psalm 19:1 (NASB): "The heavens are telling of the glory of God; And their expanse is declaring the work of His hands." I cannot see, feel, or touch God, but He is here and addressing me through nature. He is reminding me that He is amazing, powerful, and awesome and that He wants to share an intimate relationship with me. Wow!

I jot these thoughts in my journal along with some questions to think about and answer as I continue. "Why am I on this hike? What am I learning as I hike to the top? How have I acted and reacted along the way? When will this come to an end? Where will I go when the hike to the top is accomplished? Who will I thank?" It's incredible to sit by the water and listen to God's sermon without words but with what He created.

God, my heart sings, "Be thou exalted forever and ever" because I know You alone are the Creator. Today, You chose to bring me to a solitary place and use Your creation to erase the pain I have felt and to assure me I am not alone. The words *thank You* seem so inadequate right now, but that's all I can think of to say. Help me find the energy and strength to get to the top of Monument Mountain, and give me rest.

Evening is approaching. I head back to camp. Nightfall comes quickly on the mountain, so I get a small fire going and fix something to eat. I pull out my map and settle in for the night. Trail Marker 31 is a few days' hike, but it looks like the path might not be so steep. My eyes are heavy, but my heart is full from my waterfall experience. I close my eyes and dream of reaching the top of Monument Mountain.

Rays of sunshine stroke my face to let me know morning has come. It was a good night of rest. I awakened the fire by blowing gently on it. I warm myself as I eat a little bit of breakfast. I feel so much more refreshed today, so I am hoping to make great progress. I continue to study the map and make a plan.

Father, it's me again. Thanks for the waterfall experience yesterday. May I be reminded as I continue of the beauty around me. You alone are worthy of all my praise in the good times and in the bad. Guide my steps today, give me extra strength, and take me safely to the next destination.

The trail is much wider. The way is still steep and strenuous, but I'm making great progress. I make frequent stops to sip water and orient myself. I never know what I will face, so it is good to know what's around me.

In late afternoon, I am at the next place to rest for the night. I am tempted to keep moving since I have extra daylight and a spring in my step. I take out the map and decide to keep moving.

This is one of my better decisions. The way at times has been tricky, but I have arrived at my destination. The sun is setting, and the view is magnificent. I get a fire going before darkness envelops me. I find a place to plop down and have a bite to eat. The day has slipped by quickly, and I will call it a night. The sunset paints a vivid picture of the Creator before it drops behind its mountainous canvas.

My Father, how thankful I am for a good day of progress. I know You are watching over me and have guided my steps today. My body is tired, so I ask for a peaceful night. Thank You, God, for all You do each day.

Morning comes too quickly. I stretch and feel the warmth of the day beginning to make its way through the trees. I step out onto the trail and find the way ahead to be less rocky. I just may make it to Trail Marker 31 today. I eat a quick breakfast, pack my things, and get moving.

Trail Marker 31
April 11, 2012

I had another appointment with Dr. Willard; my tissue expander was filled with a saline solution. I left of course in pain, but not too bad. I made another appointment for April 20, 2012.

Trail markers come and go. Some cause me to linger, and others seem to push me back onto the trail. Trail Marker 31 is uneventful, so I head to the next trail marker. The path that was once wide is slowly becoming narrower. I will be looking for a place to hunker down for the night. The wind is picking up, so I must not tarry too long in one place. I put my hand in my pocket and run my fingers over the smooth stone—hope.

I have encountered rain only once on this hike; that was a horrific storm. It starts to drizzle, but I'm in a cave and have a small fire going. The flames flicker and dance. I can only imagine what critter must have been here before me. I am hoping it has found a larger home. The drizzle turns into a downpour, a liquid curtain. It seems just when I'm making progress, God makes other arrangements. Nothing to do but call it a night, and that is exactly what I do.

Morning brings fog, a dense one. I won't be moving from here for a while. I reread my journal. It is hard to think I have been here on Monument Mountain for six months. Each page is a powerful reminder of where I started, where I have been, and where I am going. The fog is like a roadblock. It hinders me from leaving. It controls time. I stir up the fire and stare blankly into it. I don't enjoy roadblocks. I guess I am to lay low for now. I'm sure the fog will lift soon and I'll be on my way.

Midday. The fog is lifting. I get onto the trail. The path is slippery. Getting to Trail Marker 32 will take time and energy. The mud sucking at my feet makes each step grueling. I don't get far before the rain starts pelting the trees above me. Cold and wet, I pull over to a small cleft in the rocks to wait out the rain. Of course, it keeps coming, so I decide to trudge through it as best I can. The trees are my umbrella, but the heavier the rain, the more the trees bend their leaves and dump rain on me. Ughhhh.

A very dreary day. I stop at a rock overhang. It is dry, so this is where I will try to build a fire, dry my clothes, eat a bite, and go to sleep. I hope the rain will cease by tomorrow and it will be smooth walking. The fire is warming me and drying my clothes. I close my eyes. The rhythm of the rain falling around me calms my heavy heart.

The fire is out. I am freezing, and the rain is still falling. Yuck. The prospect of another day of hiking in the rain is sheer misery. I don't feel like moving, but I must make the effort. I want to get to this next trail marker. My heart screams, *Just get to the top!* I agree with my heart.

Six months is a long time to be stuck on a mountain where the elements change quickly, the path is never straight or always wide, the tentacles of loneliness wrap their arms around me to drag me lower than I already am, and the trail is steep and rarely level. Okay, I'm guessing the picture is pretty clear. I want to scream.

I sling my backpack onto my back and set off into the pelting rain. The steady rain makes the trail slippery. The rocks and roots are bad enough, but add to them the mud. The leaves drip rain on my weary body. I strain to find the right place to walk since the water is making its own path down the trail. My shoes cannot find any place to grip, so I just slip and slide. The way is daunting. The rain continues making the path almost impassable. Rain trickles down my face and mixes with my salty tears. I want to quit.

After a day of hiking in mud, I come to a small cave. I don't care where I lay my head as long as I can get a fire going and get warm. I gather firewood for a small fire. My little place is illuminated. I see firewood stacked neatly along the wall, a place to hang my wet clothes, and a note. I unfold the paper and read,

> Rainy days are not for the faint of heart. Be very careful as you make your way to Trail Marker 32. The place where you are hiking is treacherous, and many have lost courage and turned back. Stay the course. Finish the hike. You will find what you need in your heart. You won't find it tonight, but it will come. Copy this note in your journal should you carry one and carefully place the note back where you found it because the next person who comes here will need to read these words.

I do exactly as the note says. I mull over the words and contemplate what I'll find in my heart that will make me finish the hike. Obviously, people have turned back; doing that has crossed my mind more than once. Wet, cold, hungry, and lonely pretty much sums up my last few days of hiking. I take out my map and see that Trail Marker 32 is in reach even in the rain. I stoke the fire with the wood left for weary travelers, dry my clothes, warm my body, eat something—and then it happens. Silent tears fill my eyes as they have so many times before on this journey. They burn as they inch their way down my cheeks

God, I have no words. The pain in my heart is unbearable. I'm supposed to find what I need in my heart? I can't go on. It's just too hard.

The rain is falling, but I have to move on. Trail Marker 32 is not too far away. I gather my things, but my attention is drawn to the note. I unfold it and read it once more. Are the words true? Should I keep going or turn back? My muscles ache, and I am so tired. To the right, I see Trail Marker 32. To the left, I see a way to escape trekking uphill in the mud. Turning left would allow me to call it quits. Then the words come back to my mind— *You will find what you need in your heart.*

Trail Marker 32
April 20, 2012

I had an appointment with Dr. Willard. I was hoping that my left breast would finally be equal in size to the right so I could move forward with my life. The expander was filled, but something was not right. Dr. Willard seemed as puzzled as everyone else in the room that the expander didn't look normal. He was holding my hand while Becky continued to fill the expander. He said, "That expander has a hole in it somewhere." The rest of his words vanished in the air. Tears stung my eyes. "We need some stop leak." Believe me, I would have considered it, but it wasn't legal. Amid the shock, I tried to laugh, but I was devastated. How could this be happening? Hadn't I gone through enough already? I asked what would happen now.

"We'll put the implants in. I'm not going to put another tissue expander in. I'll get Judy to schedule the surgery while you're here." Oh the tears—how they wanted to come, but instead, there was just a lump in my throat. All I wanted to do was run away. I had no words to describe my hurt. No one knew how those words wrapped sorrow around my heart.

Dr. Willard returned with a booklet showing the implant he had chosen for me and said, "This implant comes with a tube so I can fill it up if I need to … this will help make both sides even."

"Explain the tube to me," I said.

"The tube sits under the skin, not like the tubes you've had in the past. It will stick up, maybe give the appearance of a mole."

I got dressed. I was in serious pain. I went to see Judy. Her eyes said it all—no words had to be said—but when it came time to speak, her words came gently: "Your hike isn't over. There's more for you to write."

The lump in my throat got bigger. More to learn. The journey just got tougher. Surgery was scheduled for May 15. I made an appointment to see Dr. Willard on May 7. I got to the car, sat, and cried out to God. I felt so alone.

The rain continues to fall. Trail Marker 32 may be where I have to stop and camp out for a while. I don't mind stopping since the rain keeps coming. This trail marker has a couple of places to reside. I locate one only to find the same scenario as the last place—a stack of wood and a note. I realize one thing—others have passed this way without turning back. I lay my backpack down, start a fire, dry my clothes, and eat a little.

After doing my chores, I read the note.

> Dear friend, you've made it this far, so you must have listened to your heart. It tells you many things as you journey through life. Two things you should know about the heart. First, it is a wrestling place. The heart is where we fight internal battles, come to conclusions, and make decisions right or wrong. Second, it's where we connect to God in a more personal way.
>
> The journey has been tough, but you are here. You've connected with God in a deeper, more personal way. You have wrestled with your thoughts and emotions and whether you had the will to move on. I am sure it is raining as you read this as is the case with all who make it this far. To find comfort, read Genesis 8:6–11.

Someone understands what I am facing. I copy the note into my journal and replace the note. I read Genesis 8. Noah has been on the ark between nine and ten months waiting for the waters to recede. He sends out a raven to look for dry land, but the raven returns. The dove he sends out returns too. All Noah has seen for months is water in every direction. He sends another dove, and the results are different. Genesis 8:11 (NLT) reads, "This time, toward evening, the bird returned to him with a fresh olive leaf in its beak. Noah now knew that the water was almost gone."

I almost felt the boat rocking, the weariness of looking only at water, the smell of the animals, the lack of conversation or too much talking, but mainly the feeling that hope was hibernating. We have all have been on the boat with Noah at some point. We all have had our share of floods. Maybe your life has been flooded by sorrow, grief, pain, uncertainty, rejection, a spouse who stops caring, a child who goes astray, or the word *cancer*. Floods come without warning and rise in the recesses of our souls. You wait for the floodwaters of hopelessness and hurt to recede, but you wonder when that will happen.

I'm sure Noah was just as anxious as I am for the floodwaters to diminish and dry land to appear. So here comes the dove back to the ark with an olive leaf. Big deal? You bet! It meant dry land. It moved Noah from hopelessness to hope, to putting his sea legs on dry land, to watching new life begin. I long for an olive leaf. I don't have a dove, and I'm not surrounded by water and smelly animals, but I see the importance of an olive leaf. I can give olive leaves to those around me.

Olive leaves represent hope and peace. They represent us giving something we have to those who are hurting. We can all be agents of hope and peace for people struggling to find their way on their journeys. For example, the olive leaf of kind words: "There with you." The olive leaf of encouraging words: "Let's keep sharpening each other." "It's pre-cancer" "You've got some mighty good hiking boots." The olive leaf of compassion: "Your body will change, no doubt, but your life will be even richer." The olive leaf of hope: "It's only a setback, not a disaster." "He will have a mom around. Your cancer was contained. It will be okay." The olive leaf of assurance: "Whatever path God takes us on, that's how we'll go." Then I think of the olive leaf of the human touch where no words are needed, tears shared in silence, a husband who stands by you, a child who believes you are part superhero, and verses sent to calm storms in fearful souls.

This is a lot to absorb. Until tonight, I haven't realized how important an olive leaf is in my life or how important it is for me to find ways of giving olive leaves to others. When the floodwaters finally recede and I'm on dry ground, I'll be able to exclaim, "I am a flood survivor." I will have personally gone through this flood and lived to tell about it—that qualifies me to give the olive leaf of hope to someone else.

Father, what a lesson I have learned this night. Who would have thought that an olive leaf had so much meaning. I pray You will help me to be an olive leaf giver. How I praise You for all the olive leaves I have received along this strenuous hike. You have given me life. Help me never to take it lightly. Please help me remember that when the floodwaters of hopelessness were prevailing in my soul, You provided an olive leaf from Your Word to encourage and bring hope. One more thing. Bless all who have provided an olive leaf for me along the way.

The rain clouds continue to empty themselves on a saturated ground. I am taking another day here at Trail Marker 32 to journal, reflect, and pray. As I stand by the entrance of this cave, I see yet another note. I open it, and to the ground falls an olive leaf. Sleep comes much easier tonight.

In the morning, I gather my things and reflect on what I have learned from Noah. I put the olive leaf in my backpack as a reminder of my mission—completing the hike up Monument Mountain. I set out for Trail Marker 33, which is just ahead based on my map. I can reach it in a few hours given there are no setbacks or surprises.

A gentle breeze is blowing and drying the soil. The birds are singing, and I feel more at peace today. The journey has been incredibly tough at times. I had often felt like quitting, but something deep in me spurs me on. Wow! Here I am already at the trail marker. Nice spot to rest. I enjoyed the mindless hike. I know I need more days like this.

Trail Marker 33
May 7, 2012

I met with Dr. Willard to address the upcoming surgery. We talked briefly about the surgery and the implant he would use. I didn't know how I should feel. Elated I could be nearing the end of such a strenuous journey? Scared because of all the setbacks I had experienced? I felt lots of emotions all at once, and a new kind of panic gripped me. We finished talking, and I left waiting for May 15—my surgery day.

I find it unsettling how fast I arrived here today. When things run so smoothly, I get a little panicky. My life thus far has been full of paths that have been unforgiving and painful. Oh, there have been a few places where the paths were smooth, but over the past seven months, such paths have been few and far between. I scan the area where I will be staying. Not too bad, but I feel strange. Unsettled in my soul. An eerie calm surrounds me. I can't wrap my fingers around why I feel this way, but I'm sure I'll find out in time.

I do the normal things before settling in for the evening. I know this sounds silly, but I feel all alone. The aloneness presses in close to me. Each time my heart beats, it shouts, *Alone, alone, alone.* Those words mean nothing to me. I've been hiking alone for months. My mind is playing tricks on me. Maybe I'm exhausted and need to rest. I lay my head against my backpack and wait for sleep to come, but it doesn't. The word *alone* repeats itself steadily with each beat of my heart. My mind plays the game of finding other words to describe alone—*unaccompanied, unaided, by yourself, without help, abandoned, lonely, isolated, deserted, solitary.* What a pitiful list to describe the place I am emotionally in my journey.

So this is what Trail Marker 33 is all about—feeling alone. Seven months of strenuous hiking and this is where I wind up. I kick the dirt. Anger, tears, resentment, and fear surge in my soul. I kick harder at the dirt. I am so tired of being here, so tired of feeling alone at times when I need assistance, but I rarely ask for help. Again, tears are released from the dam of my soul and gush. There's no one to see them, no one to dry them, no one to encourage and guide me, no one to say, "You'll make it." No one to talk to. I'm alone.

I guess the tears had to come at some point and time. I look at the map. The trail ahead doesn't look too easy. I will stay here for another day or so, then off to Trail Marker 34. I get up and look up. The morning sun is peeking through the trees.

Dear God, I feel so abandoned. No one seems to care. Everyone is wrapped up in his or her own life. Seven months is a long time for anyone to go through pain and suffering. I have cried out to You so many times, and as I look up to the heavens, I cry out once again. I'm weary. I want to be finished. I need people to continue to be a part of my life, but that's something you can't just ask for. Speak to me, Father. The emotions, the hurt, and the pain are bogging me down. I am looking up. Make a way. Give me hope for the journey ahead.

The lack of sleep is getting to me. I cannot remember the last time I slept through the night. Time escapes me, but my thoughts are forever with me. Strange how that works. It's good to know this is not where I'll stay much longer. I rest under the shade of some trees. I witness the beauty of the sun's rays streaming down on the trail. I shut my eyes and dream of the day this hike will be finished. Oh, for that day.

I don't know how long I slept, but it was long enough to get a stiff neck. I roll my shoulders, move my neck around, and look up. The sun's rays shine on the path ahead of me. While my heart drums out the word *alone*, my spirit sinks further into despair. Even the very word sounds lonely. Silence filled the mountain. What I choose to do now will be pivotal if I were to continue on this trail.

My thoughts are not even rational. I want off this mountain. For seven months, I have walked on this journey sometimes with an overwhelming amount of guilt thinking I am the one responsible for my being here. Today, nothing has made sense. I want off the mountain. I'm ready to throw my hands up and quit. Within a split second of my irrational decision, I feel the urge to look up.

It takes only a second to be humbled in the sight of our holy God. No, I'm not looking at Him literally, but I feel His presence in a way I cannot explain. Looking up is a reminder that He has been, is, and will continue to be in control of this hiking expedition. It's a time to reflect on my attitude. I've been so busy looking around for clues that I haven't taken to time to look up.

God, my life feels like it has broken into thousands of pieces. Loneliness is tattooed in the recesses of my mind, and my heart is overflowing with pain. I often feel this assignment is too hard for me. Why did You entrust this hike to me? I'm positive You could have found someone stronger, way more spiritual—someone with better hiking shoes than mine to take on this strenuous hike. I know the trail will not get easier from this point on. I've looked up and seen Your holiness. Give me what I need today to bring You honor.

Night is upon me. I rekindle the little fire I had started earlier and get close to it. The heat makes my eyes heavy. I drift in an out of sleep until morning. It's time to push on to Trail Marker 34. Yesterday seems so long ago, and today already seems it will last forever, yet I know I must start hiking. The map indicates I will be at the trail marker today. I gather my things and head upward. The trail is steep, and my legs burn, but I have to get to Trail Marker 34. The quiet devours the world around me. I am left with my thoughts. My heart is beating loudly, but this time, it is drumming the words *Look up.*

Trail Marker 34
May 15, 2012

I faced another surgery. Dr. Willard was putting implants in and taking the tissue expanders out. Dr. Willard and I were hopeful this surgery would be the last and would give closure to this strenuous hike I had been on since October 2011.

His eyes told me the same story I was telling myself as I entered the operating room—*God have mercy*. I must have said that a hundred times before drifting off to sleep. That's all I could think of to say. My strength was gone. I asked God to have mercy on me. One more time.

Trail Marker 34 is physically draining. There is nothing in this dingy little cave. I muster all the energy I have to gather what I will need to get me through the night and morning. After the fire is going, I reorganize my backpack. Piece by piece, I take things out, and memories flood my soul.

Memories are the mirrors of the soul—they reflect what we have forgotten or choose not to see. In the dim light, I pull out my journal—my lifeline in telling my story. My Bible has sustained me and given me strength. The rocks remind me of the baggage I came with, so I write the words *Look up* on one.

I find the envelope with the olive leaf in it. Olive leaves remind me of friendships cherished, of encouraging words, and love given. I write olive leaf on another rock. It will remind me of what I am to be to others when I finish my hike. I hope soon. I am not thrilled with my circumstances, but I have a fire going. The more wood I add, the more brilliant the flame.

Life is like my small fire. When I first got here, I was bothered by all the work I had to do to start a fire. But I found that by adding small pieces of wood, the flame got brighter. So it is in life. The more olive leaves we give to others, the more hope they will find.

The trail ahead looks steep, and I am so tired physically and emotionally. As I try to find rest, my mind is occupied with the olive leaf. I guess Noah might have been at his breaking point too when the olive leaf was brought to him. God stepped in and sent the olive leaf via air mail to encourage him—a statement of hope and assurance of His promise, "I will never desert you, nor will I ever forsake you" Hebrews 13:5 (NASB). The floodwaters are receding. Hope is rising. I close my eyes as tomorrow will bring significant challenges.

Morning breaks. I stoke the fire to awaken it from its slumber. It fills the small structure with warmth. It's a good morning to plan before I continue on this trail. I get out my trail map. Wow! Since I started this journey in October 2011, I have made progress. At times, it wasn't visible, but it was happening little by little, day by day, month by month. Monument Mountain didn't look this steep when I first started. My, how far God has brought me. His grace is amazing no matter what or how I have felt these past months.

My fire's flames are hypnotizing. I wonder what plan God has for me. What will be the result of this hike? When will I get to the top of this mountain? What will be there? I find my location on the map. The next trail marker isn't too far away, but the terrain is rugged. I have enjoyed sitting, but the time has come to move forward. I am weary, but to reach the top, I must step out onto the trail.

I press forward. A few spots hinder my progress, but didn't the tortoise win the race by moving slowly and steadily? *Persistence.* I write that word on a rock. I keep moving, and within a few hours, I see Trail Marker 35. I pick up the pace.

Trail Marker 35
May 23, 2012

I saw Dr. Willard. "Everything looks great. No infection. You're healing nicely." What great words to hear from my doctor. The words *Everything looks great* were very important to me that day. I had a quote on one of my T-shirts: "A life lived in fear is a life half-lived." How true. I didn't know who had made that up, but maybe like me, they had allowed themselves to hover over the fire of fear. I was constantly wondering if indeed May 15, 2012 would be my last surgery or if the fire of fear would be ignited by the spark of infection. Those words resonated through my mind. I made an appointment for June 5, 2012, for the first filling of the left implant.

I must keep moving. No time to rest before the sun sets or I'll be trapped without shelter. It has been a good day. I have made progress, and maybe the end is in sight. The air is cool. I reach a point where I can lay my stuff down and rest for the night. I gather what I need to make the night comfortable, take out my journal, and reflect on my day.

God, I made progress today. I feel good about where I am. Physically and emotionally, I am drained. All these months of hiking have made my soul weary, but I know You are in control. Rest is what I need—Rest from the voice in me that tells me to give up, that there is no end is in sight. God, I need to know how this will bring honor to You.

It's a new day. The only things crossing my mind are the words *His grace is sufficient.* Grace is surely what I need to continue on this strenuous hike. I can make out the top of Monument Mountain from where I am, and adrenaline is coursing through my veins. I am excited to see the end. It is closer than it was seven months ago. I gather my things quickly and begin the hike to the next trail marker.

The trail is steep and harsh. It is the time of year for new growth. The trees have caught a glimpse of the sun and the color green is on the scene. All around me, trees are blooming, buds are budding, and birds are flitting here and there. The air is crisp with all the smells and sounds of spring. I'm on guard for the numerous roots and holes along the trail, which twists and turns. It's not too hot, but I feel tired, and I wonder how far my place of shelter is.

I feel invigorated by the sun shining on me. A new day dawns. I feel hope that I'll soon reach the top. I push forward wondering what it will be like to reach the end of my strenuous and long hike. I long for that day. I keep walking, but I am incredibly tired. I hear water gurgling. I keep moving until I come across a stream. The water is clear, cold, and refreshing. I drink my fill and sit on a rock. Cool, clear water rejuvenates my soul.

The scenery is breathtaking. I hadn't realized I was up so high until now. I look back at the steep, winding path and remember how it seemed so hard at times to even put one foot in front of the other. Now, my hike is almost complete. I lie on the ground and enjoy the beauty around me. That's when I see it. A small sign tacked to a tree across the stream. I cannot read what it says from here. Curiosity may have killed the cat, but it won't kill me. Off I go into the stream. The water isn't deep, and it's not cold enough to discourage me from finding out what the sign says. I slip on occasion, but I don't let my backpack get wet. It has been my survival kit for the past months, so I take good care of it.

I step on the last rock, get to the edge of the stream, and climb onto a mossy area. The sign is several yards away. I reach the tree and gaze at the sign. It contains debris collected over the winter. I take the sign down, wipe it off, and read the word *thirst*. Thirst for what? The water is refreshing. Maybe the sign is here to remind hikers how thirsty they will be if they don't rehydrate. Cute sign I suppose. I guess that's why curiosity killed the cat. I hang the sign up and see something carved on the tree—Ps. 42:1–2a.

I realize a hiker must have carved that. I knew it was from the Bible. I sit, pull out my Bible, and turn to Psalm 42:1–2a (ESV): "As a deer pants for flowing streams, so pants my soul for you, O God. My soul thirsts for God, for the living God." What was not clear to begin with is now crystal clear. I was so thirsty when I got to this point that I drank and drank the water. It rehydrated me. It rejuvenated me. It energized me.

I started journaling.

> Today, I found a sign with one word—*thirst*. I wasn't sure what it meant, but as I went to hang the sign back in its place, I saw that someone had carved Ps. 42:1–2a on the tree. I remember how tired and thirsty I was by the time I reached this spot, and when I heard the water, I picked up my pace. The sound of the water meant my physical thirst would soon be quenched. The sign was a reminder of how badly I wanted water, and the Bible verses were there to remind me to thirst after the things of God. My desire for this journey to be over has consumed me on many occasions so much so that I haven't thirsted for God as I should have. "As a deer pants for flowing streams, so pants my soul for You, O God."

To finish strong, I will have to thirst for the things of God—His way, His Word, and His wisdom. I write the word *thirst* on a rock to remind me to thirst after the things of God daily—not just when things are tough.

Night is approaching. I gather wood, get a fire going, and scoot close to it. My clothes are damp from my wading in the stream, and my body is chilled. I take out my trail map once again and see that the next several markers are close together, meaning there will be little time for rest between them. I drift in and out of sleep. The fire flickers, and the chill leaves my weary body. Rest is what I desire. Rest from the hike. Rest from this journey.

The morning sun peeks through the trees. It's time to get moving. I don't feel super energetic today, but getting to the next trail marker is a must. I stoke the fire. A little flame appears. After a while, warmth engulfs my body. I eat some breakfast and ponder the day. I reflect on yesterday's finding and how life changing that moment was for me. Just finding the stream gave me hope. I suppose this stream runs down the mountain or at least parts of it. I gather my things and press forward.

I hike for about an hour. The trail is unforgiving. I am struggling to find motivation. I want this to be over. There it is up ahead—the next trail marker.

TRAIL MARKER 36
JUNE 5, 2012

I had an appointment with Dr. Willard to start filling the left implant. It was extremely painful. After the implant was filled, Dr. Willard made me look at myself in the mirror. At that point, I hated mirrors. He said, "You'll never be the same, but I promise to do whatever I can to make you look normal in your clothes. With all the surgeries you have had, this is the best I can do."

Talk about painful words—*You will never be the same* hit me hard. I didn't need anyone to point that out to me. Every time I saw myself, I felt nauseous. I hated mirrors because they were so revealing, so truthful. I knew Dr. Willard was preparing me for the days to come when I'd have to accept my new normal. I made an appointment for July 2, 2012.

I decide to take a minute off the trail. I haven't strayed from this path since the beginning, but I need a change of scenery. To my right is a small trail that looks intriguing, so I decide to give it a whirl. I need a break from the pressure and weariness of the main trail. This trail has been so hard but in many ways rewarding. As I wind down this new trail, I want to put things in perspective, to look at things from a different angle. As I meander forward, I hear water once again. I wonder why I had never heard flowing water until now. The water had to be flowing from the top of the mountain. It wasn't gushing. Just a gentle flow.

I approach the water and remember the stream I had encountered earlier and the word *thirst.* Had I really thirsted after the things of God on this hike? Perspective. I need time to evaluate the months I spent on this trail following the trail markers obediently and never abandoning the way the map insisted I go. I need to take a look at myself and what I have learned, what I will do with this knowledge, and how I'll handle the rest of this strenuous hike. The trees bring shade and comfort to my tired body. I find a tree close to the water's edge and lean against it. I pull my journal and a new rock out. I write the word *perspective* and ask myself, *What am I really searching for by moving away from the trail?* The reoccurring answer is rest—rest from the strenuous hike and the weariness of putting one foot in front of the other. The water seems to be whispering my name, calling out to me, telling me to move closer for it is here I will learn. I move from the comfort of the shade and follow the stream. I climb on a large rock and watch the water flow over and around the rocks in its path.

The water shapes everything in its path. If a rock falls into a river, over time, it becomes a remarkable part of the scenery. The water evens out the roughness of the rock not in a day but over a long time. My emotions are all-consuming. The events surrounding the hike flashed in front of me like the rising of a curtain revealing a play. Except this is not a play, not a dress rehearsal; this is my life.

I realize why I felt compelled to move from the trail. I gain a different perspective at the water's edge. The rock is a clear representation of my life. I do some journaling.

> I am like a rock. The rock falls into the river, yet it never chooses when or even what water it will fall into, but the rock is transformed by the water; its rough edges are removed. Like the rock, I have kept moving and living. From my experiences, I am slowly becoming what God intended. I am becoming more like Him.

Leaving the trail was necessary as it gave me perspective at a much-needed time on this hike. The sun too was finding its resting place. Night was approaching. I start a small fire, which helps keep my mind in a good place. I gaze at the heavenly, starlit canvas God has placed above me. I am reminded of Psalm 147:4 (NLT): "He counts the stars and calls them by name" and Isaiah 40:26 (NIV): "Lift up your eyes and look to the heavens: Who created all these? He who brings out the starry host one by one and calls forth each of them by name. Because of his great power and mighty strength, not one of them is missing."

Not one of them is missing. Powerful words. I write them in my journal.

God, thank You for this starlit canvas—a reminder of Your splendor and glory. Thank You for helping me find my way, to find perspective, and to realize You know where I am at all times. I'm never missing from Your sight.

It doesn't seem my eyes have been shut for long before I see the sunlight spilling through the trees. It's time to find my way back to the original trail. I feel refreshed. I am more at peace, and that allows me to move at a much faster pace. Not too far ahead, I see Trail Marker 37. My heart is racing with wonder of what this trail marker has to offer.

Trail Marker 37
July 2, 2012

I had an appointment with Dr. Willard. Not too much was said—a quick visit. They removed 50 cc of liquid from the implant, and I made an appointment for August 1.

I'm moving quicker than I expected. I pull out my trail map and locate the next marker—38. It's not too far, but it appears that the terrain may change, and the heat has become unbearable. The trail is bursting with thick greenery that obstructs my view and hinders my progress. It seems that before I get started, I have to stop because of the elements. I have to retreat from the heat.

Water is in the distance. I hear it, but locating it may be difficult. The sound of moving water is barely audible, but I know it's here by all the growth around me. My preference is not to leave the path, but if that's what it takes to cool off, I'll do it. I move toward the sound of trickling water, and it's not long before I am rewarded with cool, clear water. I drink my fill and remove my socks and shoes. I submerge my feet in the cool water. Ahhh. The relief is immediate, but I can't stay here long. Relaxing isn't an option, but I take a few minutes to redirect my thoughts. *How much longer will I be forced to hike?* Doubt and fear whisper to me. Almost call out to me. The urge to quit hits me hard. I am so tired of the hiking. When will it end?

I can't allow myself to start thinking like this. I force myself to leave the refreshing, rippling water and trudge back to the trail. The trail. Familiar yet unfamiliar. Doubt and fear are walking hand in hand beside me. Taunting me. Accusing me. Consuming me. They are like shadows following me in the light and covering me when darkness prevails.

The overgrown vegetation makes me stumble and fall face-first. Frustrated and angry, I pull myself up, assess myself for injuries, and decide to find shelter. I'm beside myself for rekindling my friendship with fear and doubt. With these guys for friends, who needs enemies?

I find a place to park my weary bones. *Why now? I'm almost at the end. The hike is almost over. What's happening in me?* I ask myself. It's so hot, but it will cool down after the sun retreats behind the trees.

I go over the day's events in my mind while I gather firewood. I realize my course changed when my companions—fear and doubt—merged onto the path with me and I joined them in their shenanigans. I set up my campsite for the night and plop down in the shadiest spot I can find. I pull out my trusted journal. It sheds light on the questions my heart asks so many times.

God, so many emotions have accompanied me on this trail. Why now? Why have I allowed fear and doubt to rekindle their friendship with me? What is stopping me from moving forward? God, open my eyes.

The pages of my journal are looking worn. Many are stained with silent tears. Tears no one heard. Tears no one saw. Tears washing my soul clean of the debris left by my pain and sorrow. My journal is a stark reminder of where my feet have walked and just how long I've been trudging up Monument Mountain. I carefully study each page and call to mind every word as if I'm hearing if for the first time. I remember the pain. I rejoice over the progress.

I make a huge discovery in my journal. Fear was replaced by confidence and trust at Trail Marker 22, yet I'd subconsciously picked the rock of fear back up. For so many years, I have had the company of fear. How hard habits are to break. The sun has moved to its place of rest, and I will do the same. The air has a chill, so I build a little fire, lie down, and stare into the dark night.

God, the day has been long. Yes, I allowed fear and doubt to befriend me, and I forgot confidence and trust were at my fingertips. What do You want from me? Darkness devours me. Words escape me, Father. Please give me answers. And the strength to make it.

The sun gently rubs my face with its rays as if to say *Wake up! A new day has dawned.* I eat, grab my backpack, and traipse forward. Not too far ahead I see Trail Marker 38.

Trail Marker 38
August 1, 2012

I heard my name and went back to receive more words. "Things look fine," Dr. Willard said. "What we'll plan to do now is schedule a time to take the tube out of the implant. Let's talk about this for a minute. Understand there cannot be any more reconstructive surgery on the left side. Seven surgeries are enough, and I want to avoid infection at all cost. It's too risky. So what you see, the way you look now, is the best it will ever look on the left side. It will never look normal. I've done the best I could to make the left side match the right."

He spoke those words with such compassion but also with honesty and purity of heart. Honesty was what I'd asked for way back at Trail Marker 1.

No real words of discouragement that day. I scheduled my last surgical procedure for October 9. I didn't believe what I had just scheduled—my last appointment was on the books. I was on my way to conquering Monument Mountain. Finally, words that weren't thorny or painful. What I took away from my appointment was that I had to accept what I would look like. Nothing in the realm of normal. But the cutting-and-pasting time of my life would be over! Accept and be done—that's what I planned to do.

I strike out again moving up toward the summit of Monument Mountain. The air seems fresher, and I have a spring in my step. I feel lighter, as if a burden has been lifted. "Finally!" I say. "Good news!" Words that are alive. Words breathing life back into the torn and tattered sails of my soul. Funny what the power of a word can do. I breathe out the words ever so softly, "Not my will, but Yours, Father."

The trail has gotten steeper, and my legs are throbbing. I need to rest. I hunt for a place to set up camp. I have lots of rocks and overhangs to choose from, so finding a place to rest shouldn't be a problem. I approach a small place with a large rock jutting out over the top. "Perfect!" This place will protect me from practically every element. It's about perspective, isn't it? Just like an eagle has a proper perspective in flight, I must have a proper perspective if I want to finish this hike with fervor. I carefully set up my last campsite. Excitement overcomes me. I scratch the word *last* in the ground with a stick. Last is a powerful word. I smile, and my soul shouts, *You made it!*

A little fire does the soul good. I poke at the fire with a stick, and little embers leap from the flames and dance in the darkness. I poke at it again and again. The embers flicker for a second or two and float to the ground. The disappearing embers remind me of how hope so often has disappeared in a moment here on Eagle Height Trail. Hope, like dancing, fiery embers, have dissipated from the fire in my heart on multiple occasions on my hike. It wasn't until I stirred the ashes of my soul that hope ignited once again. Hope is burning inside me as I am finally bringing my hike on Monument Mountain to an end.

Hope. What do I hope for, Lord? Healing? Wholeness? Friendship? Spiritual Growth? Life? Father, my hope is truly in You. I ask You to shine Your light of hope through the darkness of hopelessness I have so often felt. I'm just a child, but I'm Your child. Give me strength to do what is required of me. I love You!

Rest comes easy. I inhale the word *last*, exhale the word *finished*, and sleep.

The sun makes its debut long before I do, and I feel refreshed and hopeful. I stoke the fire until the ashes come alive, make breakfast, and pull out my trail map. With my finger, I trace the outline of where Eagle Height Trail has taken me. Like arrows piercing my heart, the pain, sorrow, grief, and most of all the words come to mind.

It has been a long, excruciating hike—roots, rain, heat, fog, bruises, wind, storms, setbacks, and tears. Oh the tears that have silently etched their way down my cheeks leaving the permanent stain of remembrance. As I trace the trail with my finger, I come to the stark realization that the next trail marker is a couple of months away. The map shows the route to the top to be long and rugged. That wouldn't be so bad, but the seasons are changing. And at this elevation, weather changes quickly.

I run my finger over the map to the top and tap the spot. *Soon. Very soon*, I tell myself. I try to imagine how I will feel when I reach the top, but my mind turns quickly to the fact I will be here for a while. I need to see what natural resources I have around me and take inventory of my surroundings. I may or may not be in the safest place. The summer breeze brushes against my skin warming the desire of my heart—the desire to descend the mountain. The ascent has seemed impossible at times, the trail often impassible, but here I am getting ready to exclaim, "I'm finished!"

With the rays of sun tapping on my back, I gather firewood for the evening and decide this is a good place to stay. I have plenty of shade from the tapestry of greenery woven by the Master's hand. I have enough daylight to set out on a little excursion. I feel … maybe the word is happy. There's so much to explore. I set off with backpack over my shoulder. The birds are singing their song and I'm singing mine. Amazing how our songs though in different languages echo praise to the mighty Creator. Those birds have never carried rocks of fear, hurt, pain, or even grief around in their beaks; they just trust God to provide whatever they need and praise Him between times of provision. Okay, maybe you don't see it that way, but think—if we—all right, if I—praised Him in between times of provision, wouldn't my song be as melodious?

I am thinking about God's provision for me along this journey. The birds have no trouble praising the Creator while they look and wait for another meal, but have I praised Him for the wonderful way He has provided for me on Monument Mountain? Even during times of a drought-ful soul, He has been faithful to me. I've had a drought-ful soul more than once. Drought-fulness of the soul can be as harmful as doubt; it causes erosion of the soul that only the Living Water of Christ can restore.

Lots to learn while I'm waiting here. My journal reflects my deepest emotions and feelings I have experienced while hiking. One day, real soon, I'll write the final words in it and remember that He alone provided when the path seemed rocky and my hope was extinguished.

The birds cease their song. A warm breeze blows through the trees. Ominous clouds gather for what I believe will be a grand show accompanied by a magnificent light show in the heavens and applauded by thunder. I hear the slow rumbling of thunder rising then falling. The birds know a storm is on the way, so I quiet the song in my heart and look for shelter. Not too far away, I find a small place to wait out this storm. I scrounge around quickly, find some sticks, and make a small fire because the weather is certain to change and I need to see what's in this place. The little fire glows as does my heart. *Last* I say to myself. What a comforting word. I think of all the words I can with similar meanings—*concluding, culminating, completing, closing*—I cannot contain myself; I break out in song using the storm as my band.

It's really quaint in this little space. I wouldn't call it a cave. It's more like a tiny room. The performance of the storm is getting louder, so I figure I have time to explore this tiny room. I pull a stick from the fire. It has enough flame on the tip to allow me to scope out where I have parked myself until the storm passes. Wow. This tiny spot has depth. I carefully maneuver down the hallway and discover more tiny spaces. It's like a mini motel. Totally amazing! The flame on my stick flickers. I have to get back to the comfort of my fire. As I walk past one room, I see a little glass bottle. *What's this?* I grab it and make it back to my tiny space before the flame on my stick is nothing more than swirling smoke. A tiny bottle in a tiny space. Reminds me of a childhood story my mother used to read me. I think it was called "The Teeny Tiny Woman." I laugh.

Someone else's trash is most assuredly someone else's treasure, so I hold my little glass bottle up to the firelight. It's beautiful. I see a note inside. I remove the cork and shake the bottle until the note emerges. It reads, "The bottle you hold is only for the bold. What lurks around the corner will cause great fear, but your only job is to catch each tear."

What a silly message. What could possibly be lurking around the corner? Was this some joke a hiker thought to leave? "The bottle is beautiful," I say boldly and put the note and bottle in my backpack. The storm is making an encore performance. I'll wait until the thunder has drummed its last note and the rain takes its cue from the Master conductor before I leave. I pull the little bottle and note from my backpack and study it. My, how beautiful it is. A message in a bottle is a clever idea, but the note intrigued me even more. I repeat the poem until I can say it with my eyes closed.

I don't consider myself bold, but I did consider myself fearful. As God is my witness, I've been pretty tearful on this hike. The message in the bottle weighs heavily on my mind as I close my eyes and imagine all the things that might be lurking in the shadows. The storm ends. I hear only rain dripping from leaf to leaf. The air is cooler now that the rain has stopped.

As silly as it sounds, I am somewhat paranoid about what is lurking around the corner. I try to brush off this strange feeling, but I'm peeking over my shoulder as I hurry back to my original space. Maybe I would feel safer in the tiny space before trekking up to the Trail Marker 39, so I decide to relocate to a closed-in area. I gather my firewood and make the hike back to the tiny space. Upon arrival at my mini motel, I glimpse an eagle soaring high above. *Soar like an eagle* I jokingly think. I watch the magnificent bird fly effortlessly using the power of the gentle breeze to soar to greater heights. "Greater heights is where I'm headed, Mr. Eagle," I proclaim looking up. "I'm on the last leg of my journey, grand bird, before I too catch a gentle breeze and descend with as much grandeur as you ascend above the peaks."

I really like it here. It suits me. I get a small fire going, have a snack, and head back to where I'd found the beautiful glass bottle. I plan to take some sticks with me and build a fire in the tiny room. Who knows? I might find a note from a former hiker. I pack several sticks in my backpack and ignite another to guide me to the tiny space. The way is narrow, almost claustrophobic, but I reach my destination. I put my backpack down and rest my trusty fire stick against the wall. I get busy building a fire. Success! The room lights up. It's absolutely amazing in here.

I see words engraved on the stone. Words worn by the touch of travelers just like me. I run my fingers across the wall and touch each word, each letter. They seem to inscribe themselves across my heart. I step back and see letters carved deep into the stone that read *lachrymatory*. Long word. Makes me wish I had paid attention to the phonics lessons in elementary school. I sound it out like every good student and read what else was engraved in the stone.

> Lachrymatory—A bottle, also called during the Victorian Era a tear bottle. Tears were collected into the bottle during seasons of great loss, and then the tear bottle was placed on a mantle. Over time, the tears evaporated, which meant the mourning season was over and joy had come.

Wow. I would have filled up hundreds of those tear bottles along this treacherous hike. Amazing what grief can do to a person. Quietly and reverently, I read the words again to grasp their meaning. I run my fingers across the words *tear bottle.* At the end of the inscription are some letters and numbers—Ps. 56:8. Another verse. I couldn't wait to see what this bottle and David, the psalmist, had in common. I pull out my Bible worn and tattered from my searches for answers, help, and strength, and I read, "You keep track of all my sorrows. You have collected all my tears in your bottle. You have recorded each one in your book" (Psalm 56:8 NLT).

God has caught all my tears. He's kept track of all my sorrows.

O God, I don't understand why You love me the way You do, nor do I understand why You care enough to gather my tears. Yet You have collected them one by one. You didn't miss any. You recorded each one in Your book so in due time I would find comfort and relief. I need You, Father, to help me with this last trek, to renew my spirit, to strengthen my soul, and to get me to Trail Marker 39 safely. I'm ready for all this to be over.

I pull out the tear bottle. It's so small. It has a bluish tint, and around the opening is a lip that fits to the corner of your eye. I guess this is what allows the tears to flow into the bottle. And a little cork. They must have cried a lot during the Victorian Era to come up with this idea of crying into a bottle. And one so tiny. I giggle as I imagine feeling the urge to cry and running to get my tear bottle. The things I find to amuse me. Exploration Mini-Motel Room 1 is a success, and I meander back to my tiny space for the night.

I give the fire a gentle stir, and the embers glow. Before long, the flames are reaching up, and I think about the tear bottle and the message it contained. I write the word *tears* on a smooth rock.

The morning chill shakes me awake. I realize time has flown as I have hunkered down in my mini motel. I have explored every crevice and found five little rooms, but only one room had a word for me. I examine my map. I place my finger on my location and see I'm only about a week out before I reach Trail Marker 39. I know God gave me this wonderful place to stay these past months, provided me all I needed, and taught me numerous things, but it's time to finish my hike on Monument Mountain.

One week. Rough terrain. Weather changing. New season. Snow. Frustration. Despair. Discouragement. I want to quit. The wind has picked up speed, and the air seems to have the ability to freeze the words I speak aloud to myself. The trail is slippery. I cannot begin to count the times I have fallen, but I'm determined to reach Trail Marker 39. I have to stop. My body has been pushed to its limits. There are very few places to stop and rest. Building a fire is virtually impossible. Every part of my body is cold

God, can You hear me? I'm cold. Miserable. Exhausted! Did I mention cold? I want to lay my head down and sleep. I've walked for days with very little rest. Why did You make it so hard? I'm cold and need a place to rest.

My body shakes from the chilling wind. Snow is beginning to gently fall. *One more day* I tell myself as I pull my knees up under my chin. One more bone-chilling night and I'll reach my destination. I pull my journal out and with shaking hands I scrawl,

> Determination is nothing more than willpower. Determination means not giving up no matter how bad I want to run down this mountain. Determination is simply this—stick-to-it-tive-ness. I'm learning a lot about myself and my will. I want to quit, yet I want to finish. I realize I cannot claim mountaintops unless I am willing to endure the hike. Determined to reach Trail Marker 39.

Trail Marker 39
October 9, 2012

That was my big day. My last surgical procedure would entail taking out the tube. I'd have to deal with whatever the outcome was. I'd never look normal, but I believed that over the last couple of months, I had come to terms with the words Dr. Willard shared.

Rosa and I planned to have a great celebratory lunch after this, and then I'd enjoy another one with my family.

My name was called, and I went back. Dr. Willard and I discussed that once the tube was removed, it would all be over. He numbed the area, made a small incision on my left side, and gave a gentle tug. I could not express the joy I would be feeling in a few minutes. I'd be set free from this crazy tube and could experience some normalcy.

He tugged one more time and then it happened. Every facial expression in that room changed from joy to sadness. I knew something had happened. Dr. Willard said, "I haven't seen that happen in twenty years." *Seen what?* I wondered. "The tube snapped in half. The other half is somewhere in you. We'll have to do emergency surgery."

He stitched the incision. The tears came. I sobbed uncontrollably. I didn't care who watched. I had come completely to the end of myself. Dr. Willard came back into the room. Wise words were spoken with such compassion and confidence: "I can't explain it. I just know it happened for a reason. God has a plan, but I don't know what it is. On the flip side, this could be really for the better. I can fix what didn't look right."

I made an appointment for another surgical procedure on October 11, 2012.

God, Your yoke is *not* easy. Your burden is *not* light! Why couldn't I just enjoy the word *last*? I obeyed You when You put me on this strenuous trail. It's been more than one person should have to handle. I've faced loneliness daily. Been eaten alive with fear on multiple occasions. Prayed when I had no words left to utter. Cried countless tears. Only to experience this. Do You see me as a useless vessel? Why, God? Why?

Stunned at the change in the terrain on Eagle Height Trail, I decide I must rest and refuel my energy. I sit under a tree that has succumbed to its appointed season and obediently dropped its leaves. I press my back against the trunk, pull out my journal, and write.

> Little trusted journal. Right now, I thought I would be writing the final words on your page. But no, that didn't happen. I am sitting here looking at the scenery. So many trees have lost their leaves. They sit barren waiting on a new season, yet their roots are planted deep in the ground, roots reaching into the depths of the ground making it firmly planted regardless the season it faces. A new season is what I long for. And roots that go deep to withstand the seasons of life.

With these words penned, I place my journal in my backpack. As I slip it into its appointed place, I feel my little tear bottle. I take it out and place it in my pocket as a reminder that tears are for a season.

I start to walk. As I trudge, trip, grab, and complain, the snow falls like confetti. Earlier and earlier every day, the sun runs behind the trees and darkness consumes me. I have to stop, find a way to make a fire, and rest. Tomorrow, I will set out for Trail Marker 40 and whatever it brings.

Shivering and exhausted, I pass by an overhang. It looks dry enough. Now to find some dry wood so I can at least get warm. I find a few sticks and remember I have some sticks tucked away in my backpack from my last adventure. I gather as much firewood as I can—breaking off small limbs from the surrounding trees—and start my little fire. While the fire is warming my body, my soul feels cold. I put more wood on the flames so I don't lose the fire. My emotions take on the darkness of the night, and words like stars begin popping out radiantly revealing just who I am in the dark.

Bitterness. Sadness. Anger. Fear. Doubt. Discouragement. Hopelessness. Failure. Drought. Depression. All these words stare at me reminding me of the struggles I have faced on Eagle Height Trail. They light up the night, and for the first time, I really feel I cannot make it. I wonder why I am alive after all the setbacks and struggles I have faced. I watch the flames. Bitter words, death words light up the sky like fireworks. Words … isn't this what my hike has been all about? Ultimately, there has been power in every word I have heard over the past twelve months. Words of life. Words of death.

The fire is crackling. I look for a place to rest. I wonder how many other hikers have found themselves in this spot. Obviously a lot. I notice how many rocks were piled up. Rocks are lying all around. Rocks left behind. Probably used to provide heat or contain their fire. I am reminded of the rocks I carry in my backpack. Rocks I have toted many miles. I unzip my backpack and take out my smooth rocks.

My rocks remind me where my feet have trod on this journey. Then a still, small voice whispers in my heart, *Your hike cannot be finished until you give me your all.* My all? What does this mean? I have given everything I have to finish strong. *I want it all.* The voice is stronger and louder in my heart.

Well, Father, I sit here by this fire watching the embers glow. My emotions are high. My thoughts are running wild. My heart is heavy. Yet You say "I want it all." Haven't I given my all?

I lean against a stone. *I want it all.* Clearly, that's what I heard in my heart. No matter how hard I search the innermost part of my being, I struggle with the word *all.* I've always understood all to mean all. I search my mind for other words with a similar meaning. I come up with *solely, utterly, entirely, each and every.* "Each and every," I whisper.

Then it hits me. The only rock I have given up thus far is fear. I start to dig inside my backpack and pull out eleven rocks written on with invisible yet permanent ink of the soul. "Soul ink," I whisper into the darkness. What does soul ink look like? I believe it's the memories, loss, hurt, pain, and grief graffitied on our hearts. Sometimes our soul ink seems impossible to erase because these emotions and feelings have been such an intricate part of our journey. We own them and really somehow believe that if we allow them to be removed, that will cause more pain. The rocks I have refused to leave behind are stained with indelible soul ink. Bitterness. Depression. Despair. Setback. Failure. Hopelessness … the list goes on and on. I place them in a pile.

My silent tears have come to life. And yes, I catch them in my tear bottle. They're a reminder that not all tears have to be silent. And the permanent ink I used to write words of pain, hurt, loss, and grief on my soul can be erased and changed when I release every one of them to my Lord and Savior. The words *each and every* jog my memory back to the word *all.* "All," I say. And for the first time since I have been on this strenuous hike, the tears flow easily. I sob.

Father, how foolish I have been to cling to words of destruction. Heavy words I have carried all this way. Rocks bearing invisible words written with soul ink. Words only You can erase and replace with words of hope. I don't want to own these death words any longer. So Father, as painful as it is, because they have been part of my journey for twelve months, here they are. Forgive me for doubting and questioning Your guidance. The weight I have carried is of my own doing. Take the rocks that have caused me to stumble and replace them with Your words. You are my Rock.

Morning has come. I'm on the way to Trail Marker 40. I see the red marker in the distance and with urgency approach it only to find I must travel over a narrow bridge to reach the summit. It's wide enough for only one person to cross, which means one never meets anyone coming back on it. Either I cross it or turn around and go back down the mountain. I have to decide. My backpack is lighter as I no longer carry the heavy rocks. I consider my options. The bridge goes straight up. It looks rickety. I'm sure that many have walked away from this part of the trail but that others have taken one step of faith and started the journey to the summit. I take one step onto the bridge. It creaks and sways. Fear grabs at my feet telling them to turn back, but I am determined. Slowly and methodically, I put one foot in front of the other until my feet hit Trail Marker 40.

Trail Marker 40
October 11, 2012

Dr. Willard did the surgery. He replaced the broken implant with a new one. He was able to make my left side look somewhat normal. He was pleased with the outcome, and so was I.

The summit. I have finally made it. I pull out my last smooth rock and write the word *survivor.* I take all the smooth stones out and set them up in the order in which I wrote them. *Confidence and Trust. Faithfulness. Hope. Courage. Friendship and Family. Look Up. Olive Leaf. Persistence. Thirst. Perspective. Tears. Survivor.* I look at them. Each word tells a story of my journey. Just as God told Joshua to take twelve stones from the Jordan and build a memorial, a place to remember that God stopped the flow of the Jordan River when the ark of the covenant went across it (Joshua 4:21–24), my twelve stones will be a memorial set up in my heart and mind as a testament to what God has done in my life. They will be a reminder of God's provision to my son, my husband, my friends, and others hikers.

I bow prostrate on the cold, summit rock.

If it were not for Your grace, strength, and guidance, I wouldn't be here. I understand, Father, that many have forged their way through devastating hikes only to find they couldn't trust the bridge. The narrow bridge was built by the Carpenter's hands, and though I felt unsure and scared as I crossed it, faith had me by the hand and gently guided me. You, dear Father, whispered in my heart, *My burden is light* and *I will never leave you or forsake you.* You cheered me and comforted me when my strength was depleted. Lord, let me never forget the lesson of the narrow bridge.

There are no words to describe what I feel as I gaze across the scenery here atop Monument Mountain. I see in the distance a lone hiker coming up this strenuous trail. I pray whoever it is will find the nooks and crannies of this mountain and find the things I left behind to encourage others.

As I continue to look around this peak, I see something inscribed on a tablet, words possibly written by someone who has shared the pain and endured this strenuous trail and now bears the scars.

> Never be ashamed of the scars that life has left you with. A scar means the hurt is over, the wound is closed, you endured the pain, and God has healed you.

Before I leave, I write those words in my journal. In the quiet of the moment, I hear an eagle cry out above. I am reminded that I can soar like an eagle. I lift my hands in praise and at the top of my voice yell, "It is well with my soul!"

I will stay here a little longer and worship the One who blazed the trail for me. As I look back over at the narrow bridge, a gentle wind begins to blow. I place my hands in my pocket only to find my little tear bottle. I take it out and hold it up to the sun. My tears have evaporated. My time of mourning is over. Joy had finally come.

I gather my rocks and speak each word as I carefully place them in my backpack. I remember the time and the place when I wrote the words. I open my journal one last time and pen these words.

> Today, I reached the final trail marker of my journey. I never want to forget the lesson of the narrow bridge, nor do I want to forget the meaning behind each of the twelve smooth stones I carry in my backpack. Most important, I want to remember to pass along the olive leaf to those who will have their own mountain to hike.

Dear reader,

I never set out to write or publish a book. The pages you have read were penned during some of my darkest days. I started to journal the day I heard the words "You have cancer." Journaling my journey gave me an outlet, a voice to share my fears, hurts, pain, and grief. Writing was the only way I could wrap my mind around what was happening. The more I wrote, the more I saw God teaching me things I needed to change. I found out that the darkness revealed the true me, and I didn't like what I saw. So I set out to be teachable. I wanted to change.

What I have found most interesting is that the hike ends at Trail Marker 40. Forty has great significance in the Bible; it represents a time of testing. Believe me, I was tested sometimes beyond what I thought I could bear. As the words continued to flow from my heart onto paper, I realized other hikers would find themselves on a similar trail and hence this book, *Silent Tears.*

I appreciate the time you have spent reading my words. I pray they have given you life—life to continue your hike no matter the trail God has put you on. I pray you will release the extra weight, those heavy rocks, and replace them with words of hope. I also pray you will allow God to erase the invisible soul ink you may have used to condemn yourself for the situation you are in. Allow your silent tears to come to life because joy really does come in the morning.

Don't make your darkest hour your defining moment.

I thank my heavenly Father, who provided me with the ability and desire to journal my journey. My husband, Brian, and my son, Jonathan, deserve a huge thank-you for walking alongside me during this season of my life. Their hike wasn't easy either!

My parents, who so believed in this book, have been prayer warriors and caretakers who have supported me during every surgery and all the words spoken to me.

Thanks also to my dear friends and their families, friends who provided words of encouragement, and neighbors who brought meals and took Jonathan to school.

I would be remiss if I didn't thank Dr. Willard and his staff for all the care given to me on this strenuous hike. You all hold a special place in my heart! Thank you for all you do for those like me who will face journeys of their own.

Printed in the United States
By Bookmasters